MW01234201

IN THE SHADOW OF DEATH

IN THE SHADOW OF DEATH

A Young Girl's Survival in the Holocaust

Miriam Kominkowska Greenstein

Afterword by Marshall M. Lee

PRESS-22

PORTLAND, OREGON

In the Shadow of Death has been edited and designed by John Laursen at Press-22, and printed by Millcross Litho. The paintings reproduced here were created by Miriam Greenstein in 1994 and 1995.

ISBN 978-0-942382-00-6

Press-22
4828 Southeast Hawthorne Boulevard
Portland, Oregon 97215

ACKNOWLEDGMENTS

Many people have provided encouragement for this endeavor, including all the middle-school and high-school students who have asked, "When can I read your book?" I want to thank my cousin Merle Greenstein for his unwavering moral support, and for his insistence that I publicly display my paintings. I am also grateful to Steve Graham for his thoughtful assistance.

My heartfelt gratitude to Dr. Marshall Lee for reviewing the manuscript and offering helpful suggestions, and for writing the essay that concludes this volume. I am deeply honored to have an afterword from the author of the magnificent history text that graces the wall of the Oregon Holocaust Memorial.

Last and most important, my sincere thanks to John Laursen, my dear friend, editor, and publisher, without whose expert guidance this book would never have come to fruition.

In Memoriam

My parents, Zalmen Kominkowski and Ruta Kominkowska
My maternal grandparents, Zigmund Jakubowski and Helenka Jakubowska
My paternal grandparents, Menahem Kominkowski and Hinda Kominkowska

This book is dedicated to my daughters, Ruth, Helena, Audrey, and Cathy, who have brought an incredible amount of joy into my life. They are my reason for being, and for my speaking out against prejudice and hatred. I speak because I want a more loving and accepting environment for my grandchildren, Kim, Julie, Steven, Kelsey, Stephanie, and Nathan, and for my great-grandchildren, Alexis, Tahvia, and Giselle.

Contents

Prologue

Don't Talk About It!

1945–1998

I had somehow managed to stay alive through three years of slave labor in the Łodz ghetto, deportation to Auschwitz, and the horrors of Auschwitz and Bergen-Belsen. I was shipped from Bergen-Belsen to a slave-labor camp in Magdeburg, Germany, and then back again to Bergen-Belsen. I was liberated on the 15th of April, 1945.

When Germany invaded Poland in 1939 I was a nine-year-old child about to start the fourth grade. Life was wonderful. I thrived on the love that surrounded me. As an only child—and as the sole grandchild on my mother's side of the family—it felt as though I was always the primary focus of their pride and love. Upon liberation, at age fifteen, I had no home, no family, no country. I searched Red Cross lists for family members who might have survived, but to no avail. There was no one left. I alone remained.

I had only one hope: to find my mother's brother, Maurice Jacobi —Uncle Moniek—and his wife, Hanita, in the United States. I remembered him from my childhood. He and Mother were very close, and I adored him. He had emigrated in 1938 to marry his American sweetheart in Portland, Oregon. Uncle Moniek was to be our central contact outside of Europe if the war ever ended. In case of separation we were to get in touch with him.

I had had my uncle's address drilled into me. I wrote to him, but, after several unanswered letters, I was in despair. Just about when I was ready to give up hope of ever hearing from him, I received a telegram. Only one of my letters had reached him. By then I was in a displaced-persons camp in Sweden.

Uncle Moniek and Aunt Hanita were determined to get me out of Europe and to bring me to the United States, and in doing so accomplished what seemed impossible. After being told that it would take five years to get me out, they did it in a scant few months. On November 26, 1945, I arrived in New York aboard the Norwegian America Line's SS *Stavangerfjord*, disembarked, and was reunited with my beloved uncle.

My Aunt Hanita immediately became known to me as "Ciocia"—Polish for "Auntie." She was on a mission to make me into an American teenager before we boarded the train to Portland, and some of my earliest memories of this country are of shopping with her. The first project was proper underwear. That meant a bra, among other things, which was a mystery to me, since I was flat as a board and totally underdeveloped. Poor Ciocia—she and Unkie were childless and really had no clue what a teenager should wear. I was allowed to pick out my own coat, a blue, wool, three-quarter-length job trimmed with Persian lamb. Wedgie shoes and a fancy hat completed the outfit. I was now beautifully attired. Oh yes, lipstick and other cosmetics were the final touch. I felt so sophisticated, without the slightest idea that I was wearing clothes fit for an elderly—or at least middle-aged—matron. The clothes might actually have been just fine in Europe, but they were totally inappropriate for an American teenager. The mid-1940s was the age of "sloppy-joe" sweaters, pegged skirts, bobbie socks, and Armishaw saddle shoes or penny loafers.

After the first day, Unkie refused to go shopping with us. Ciocia and I were on our own. She spoke only English, and though I spoke fluent Polish and German and a little Swedish, I had only a few words of English. We communicated with gestures and head nods. It worked. We had our own language of love. I adored her and she loved me.

Oh, the wonderful feeling of belonging! From that first reunion in New York, and continuing during our life in Portland, whenever my wartime experiences came up, Unkie said, emphatically, "Don't talk about it!"—and I was not about to upset the apple cart. I could not displease either one of them. So when Unkie said, "Don't talk about it," I did exactly that. My immediate past, those five nightmare years, could now exist only in my mind. Somehow my life in the camps became something to be ashamed of, almost as though it had been my fault. Only my stories of a wonderful childhood life prior to the war could be told and retold. Speaking of things that had happened during the war was absolutely taboo. None of my friends ever asked questions about my parents or family. Living in a world of silence, I worked very hard at becoming an average American teenager—trying to be a good student, to have fun, and, most important, to be liked and accepted.

Of course, my foreign accent set me apart. More than anything, I wanted to speak proper English and get rid of my accent. One day I became aware that I was thinking in Polish and translating into English. Everything seemed to get mixed up and lost in the translation. I forced myself to think in English, and that made a tremendous difference. My English rapidly improved. I was attending an all-girl high school. The principal, my teachers, and the other students were wonderful and very kind to me. It may seem hard to believe, but in 1946 I was the only non-English-speaking student in the entire school. There were no special classes. I had to sink or swim.

Life was good. I made many friends, loved all my studies, and couldn't get enough education. I was sixteen when I arrived in Portland. My formal education in Poland had ended with the third grade. I was obsessed by my desire to graduate from high school on time, at the age of eighteen. To my American teachers it seemed impossible. To me it was a goal that I had to meet. And I did, graduating from Grant High School in June of 1948, four months before my nineteenth birthday. Pretty good for a foreign kid who barely spoke English when she started school.

I thought that I was college-bound, but love intervened. Toward the end of 1946 I met a very attractive young man. His name was Tole Greenstein. Tole had served in the Pacific, and, having been discharged from the army, was attending college on the GI Bill. He invited me to a formal dance and from then on I never dated another man. We fell madly in love and went steady for close to a year. He asked me to marry him, and I was thrilled to accept his proposal. Three months after I graduated from high school we were married. I wanted to continue my education, and Unkie and Ciocia pleaded with me to wait until I had a college degree before getting married. They told me that I was too young, that if it was true love it would endure.

They were right, of course, but I couldn't wait. I had this enormous need to start a family—to have children who were my own flesh and blood, and thus to rebuild our family and, in a sense, to defeat Hitler myself. I was very fortunate. Despite some doctors' dire predictions that I probably could never conceive, let alone carry to term, I gave birth to four beautiful healthy baby girls. Ruth was born on September 22, 1949; Helena on September 1, 1951; Audrey on January 29, 1954; and Cathy on March 2, 1957. They were, and still are, my pride and joy, the main reason for my existence.

Tole knew that I was a concentration-camp survivor. By then, though, my uncle's firm injunction—"Don't talk about it!"—was deeply entrenched within me, so ingrained that I could not even share my history with my own husband, and he never asked.

I loved my life. It was everything I had dreamed of: beautiful children, a loving husband, and a home of our own—a life full of friends, parties, and travel. Unkie and Ciocia adored the girls, and were wonderful grandparents. Tole was very involved in his optometric practice. He specialized in developmental optometry, dealing primarily with children who had vision-related learning disabilities, and developed an international reputation in his field. Besides being a room mother and a Bluebird leader, I was involved in the Oregon Optometric Auxiliary, and after many years of service became the state president. I was also very active in Women's American ORT — Organization for Rehabilitation through Training, a nonprofit group dedicated to fighting poverty by providing vocational training to youth and adults — serving as president and on the national board. And the list goes on. I was outgoing and gregarious, and loved to entertain; I didn't need much of an excuse to throw a party. Yet no matter what I did, deep down inside I felt extremely isolated. The term "Holocaust" had not yet been coined, or at least I had never heard it used. "Holocaust survivor" — what's that? So I ignored the pain, continuing to party hearty, drink, smoke, and dance the night away. Still, no matter what I did, the nightmares were always there.

Eventually the reality of my experiences crept out of the shadows, and hit me full blast. In the middle of a hot summer night a local fireworks factory went up in flames. Even though it was almost five miles away, it shook our house. The roar and thunder of exploding fireworks woke me up. According to Tole, I sat up in bed, screaming. "They're killing my babies! Oh my god, they're killing them!" I had no memory of that night. I only know what Tole told me. He couldn't calm me down, so he took my hand and led me to their bedrooms. He said later that I touched each one of their faces, saw that they were OK, and let out a deep sigh of relief. The whole time he kept saying, "See, they are fine. They're sleeping peacefully." Afterwards I went to the bathroom and vomited. The next morning, Tole asked, "Are you alright? How do you feel?" I was puzzled by his questions. "What do you mean? I am fine, of course," was my immediate response. As he told me what had happened, I was stunned.

I had no memory of the incident, but it was the first crack in my armor. Through the ensuing years I had multiple occasions of bizarre behavior. Every so often — I never knew when it would hit, but it was usually after a few drinks—I would land in the bathroom, vomiting and regressing back to my time in Auschwitz. It was always something to do with my mother. Tole never understood what was really going on. He would be very angry at my behavior, and I let him believe that it was the alcohol.

One night we went to dinner with a visiting psychologist, a close friend of Tole's, but someone I had not met before. Something triggered me, and I proceeded to tell him my whole life story. Tole was stunned. He couldn't believe that I had just spilled out my life to a relative stranger. It was a first for me, and it was the first time that my husband had ever heard me talk about the war and the concentration camps. After that night, although there was still no discussion of it between us, he became more aware of my private hell. Sometimes he would say to me, "You had a bad night again. You were screaming and crying. I couldn't understand you. You were speaking in a foreign language." I imagine that I was speaking Polish.

By this time there were a handful of books published about the "Holocaust." Oh, yes. The world had found a word for all the atrocities. *Holocaust.* I devoured those books, reading straight through the night. I would cry and swear, but, no matter what, I couldn't put a book down until I read the last page. I was verifying my memories: *Yes, yes! It really did happen! I do remember. It's not just a recurring nightmare. Those things did occur.* To a certain degree I am still doing this. Verifying, finding the dates, nightmares and dreams all running together. After reading through the night I would get up, put on my happy American-mother-wife face, and tend to the mundane everyday rituals of a happy housewife. I accumulated quite a library of Holocaust literature, but still I allowed myself very little conversation about my past life. I told my girls many stories about my life in Poland, but somehow they all ended before my tenth birthday.

One of the books in my collection was *Eva*, by Meyer Levin. Helena, my second-oldest daughter and a voracious reader, was in the seventh grade. Unbeknown to me, she had decided to read *Eva*. One evening, while the two of us were standing at the kitchen sink making a salad, she set about telling me the story of Eva, an eighteen-year-old Polish Jewish girl in German-occupied Poland. My daughter was very proud of her knowledge of a subject that she was sure her socialite mother could not possibly know about or understand. When I quietly responded, "If you want to know more about it, or have questions, just ask me," she was outraged. "What do you know about it?" she spat out at me in a disparaging tone. "I was there," was my simple reply.

After that incident I broke the silence. Although still not speaking of it publicly, I shared many stories with my girls. Usually it was Helena who would open the subject, and we spent many late evenings talking into the dawn hours, carrying on the mother-daughter dialogue, me sitting up in bed with her perched at the foot of it.

Still, the nightmares continued. Most of the time I did not remember much, but the king-size bed often looked like a battlefield, a physical sign of my tortured nights.

Tole died in March 1985, following an eight-month battle with brain cancer. He was sixty years old and I was fifty-five; we had been married for more than thirty-six years. Now my life was turned upside down once again, and, although I was comforted by my daughters, the old familiar pain of being alone was pervasive. I became a real-estate agent, and kept myself very busy during evenings and weekends, the loneliest parts in a single person's life.

Eventually, Helena suggested that I write my life story. I wrote and wrote, wrote and rewrote. We were going to put it into a manuscript, but we never managed to pull it all together. As time went on, it seemed less important, because I had discovered and joined the fledgling Oregon Holocaust Resource Center. The Center had a speakers bureau and I signed up to be one of the speakers, sharing my story with middle-school and high-school students who otherwise might understand very little about World War II and the Nazis, let alone know about the terrible events of the Holocaust.

In the early 1990s, a group of local Holocaust survivors organized a broad coalition of civic and religious organizations in the Portland area to build an Oregon Holocaust Memorial in Portland's Washington Park. A group of five of us, all Auschwitz survivors, were charged with the sacred mission of returning to Europe to collect soil from the Nazis' six main extermination camps — Auschwitz, Treblinka, Majdanek, Chelmno, Belzec, and Sobibor — all of them in Poland. Half a century after the camps were liberated, the soil in them still contained a heavy mixture of human ashes and bone fragments. With legal permits from the governments of both the United States and Poland, we set out on a journey to gather soil from each of the killing camps.

It took a decade to design our memorial, and to raise the money to build it. The six bags of soil and ash that we had brought back with us were placed in a tightly sealed vault that is interred at the base of the memorial wall. The Oregon Holocaust Memorial was dedicated on the 29th of August, 2004.

Returning to Poland

*"Why am I going back to Poland? Do I have to? The others can do it with-
out me." "OK, accept it. You have a need to do this." "But I am scared."
"Scared of what?" "Scared of the pain of going back to nothing. I know that
this trip will in part be a search for myself — for the little girl who once was,
and who ceased to exist."*

*For months, this silent argument raged within me. I can't do this,
but I must do it. I can't go, yet I must go. At last it became crystal clear
to me that even though, in theory, I had a choice, in fact I did not. I had
to go. I needed to participate in this mission, no matter how painful and
psychologically charged.*

*By the time we left Portland, our group had grown from five travelers
to fifteen, including two more Holocaust survivors. We became a close-knit
family, supporting each other throughout this powerful and emotionally
fraught experience. I had invited my four daughters to join me, and had
added sightseeing trips to the places of my childhood. I wanted my children
to know their heritage, to see where their maternal family had lived, and to
understand what had formed me as a person. Once my girls were involved,
going back to Poland became reasonable, even exciting. There was no more
ambiguity. It seemed, now, beshert — inevitable.*

*As word of our trip got out, it captured the imagination and interest
of the local news media. And so, in 1998, on the last day of April, our group
departed Portland amidst a great fanfare of television cameras and inter-
views. Fifteen hours later we landed in Warsaw, Poland.*

Chapter One

SOMPOLNO, RADZIEJOW, ALEKSANDROW

1929–1939

My father's family lived for generations in Sompolno, the Kominkowski family home base. Dad's father, Menahem Kominkowski, owned a huge lumber mill in Sompolno. I have vague memories of the mill, which had a rail siding on the premises, and to a little kid seemed enormous.

My father was the third child and first-born son, one of seven siblings; he had two older sisters, Sarah and Berta, three younger brothers, Icek, Jakub, and David, and a younger sister, Ciesia. Grandpa Menahem and Grandma Hinda had a very large house on the town square, which was the gathering place for my father's family. I recall all the laughter and fun—there were so many of us, and I loved being with all my cousins. To my dad and his brothers and sisters, even for those who moved away, Sompolno was always home.

We moved to Radziejow when I was still quite young—perhaps three or four years old—but my parents and I continued to return to Sompolno for family celebrations. We went for Passover Seders, for other holidays, and for Aunt Ciesia's wedding. Grandpa Kominkowski was a very pious and observant Jew, and the Seders dragged on and on; it seemed like hours while Grandpa read every word in the Haggadah and recited all the prayers. All of this was in Hebrew. Neither I nor my cousins Lydzia, Juziek, Heniek, and Tusia understood a word of Hebrew; nevertheless we had to sit quietly and listen respectfully to the whole service. After many, many prayers the food was served and we were permitted to talk, even to wiggle around in our chairs. My favorite part of the Seder was hiding the *afikomen* and singing the traditional Passover songs.

Aunt Ciesia's wedding was a totally different kind of event. The celebration began days before the actual ceremony, with relatives and friends arriving daily from nearby towns and far-away cities. They all brought their children. My cousins and I had tons of kids to play with; we felt very important since it was all happening at our grandparents' house. We were the hosts! The tables overflowed with food and sweets, and there was music and dancing for all ages. I don't remember how, why, or exactly when, but sometime during that week-long celebration my cousins and I, along with a few other kids, went down to the cellar. There we discovered many barrels of homemade cherry wine. In Poland—or maybe it was more of a Jewish custom—everyone made wine, and cherry was at the top of the list. Of course, to make wine the barrel had to be chock-full of cherries, which fermented with sugar and turned into wine. Those cherries were utterly delicious, and on many prior occasions I had eaten a few. This time, with no adult supervision, we gorged ourselves on the cherries and got a little drunk. I don't recall any punishment, just being sent to bed. To this day, whenever I remember that occasion I have a very warm fuzzy feeling of family, love, fun, and togetherness.

Radziejow. . . . At the simple mention of the name, childhood memories come flooding back in magnificent Technicolor. I can still picture our house and lumberyard, as well as the long walks to school and the main part of town with its town square way up on the hill. We lived down below, on the outskirts of town at the beginning of acres and acres of fragrant farmland, full of rich golden fields of wheat dotted with wild poppies and deep-blue cornflowers. Those were the sights and smells of summer. In the winter the same fields rested under a heavy blanket of pristine white snow. To me Radziejow was an absolute wonderland.

The Kominkowskis were a lumber-business family. The lumberyard and building-supply business in Radziejow was jointly owned by my father and his brother-in-law, my uncle Stasiek. Our home and the business office were situated in one building. We had two entrances—a formal one from the street and another through the lumberyard, past the office and directly into the kitchen. Even though it was a much longer walk, I preferred going all the way around through the lumberyard entrance to backtrack into the house.

The smell of freshly cut wood and sawdust, and the landscape of huge stacks of lumber forever shifting and changing, always managed to thrill me. I never got tired of it. As the lumber was sold throughout the day, the crisscrossed stacks would diminish. Quite often the workmen would intentionally pull out boards from the center, which created open spaces inside the stacks that were absolutely perfect for me and my playmates to design an imaginary home with rooms, and sometimes even a grocery store. Life was always an adventure.

Uncle Stasiek and Aunt Sarah lived on the other side of the lumberyard. They had two children, Lydzia, a year older than I, and Jusiek, a year younger. We were the three musketeers, always adventure-bound and often in trouble. Oh, how I loved them, my two companions. Lydzia was everything I wanted to be but never could. She had ink-black hair, wore beautiful school uniforms, and in my eyes was the most lovely girl in our school. Jusiek was the kid-brother and younger-cousin pest. We graciously tolerated him. I was short and stocky, with chestnut-colored hair and a school uniform that to me never looked as glamorous as Lydzia's. Without a doubt I was the tomboy and daredevil of our little group.

I will never forget our winter sledding adventures, the sleigh rides with our parents, and the wonderful summer days of picnics in the woods. We went with our mothers in horse-drawn carriages to nearby farms for lazy afternoon teas under sun-drenched rose arbors. The farm women served us delicious homemade cookies, the best cherry turnovers I've ever had in my life, and luscious, ripe, freshly picked fruit. Later on, while our mothers visited, we kids played in the wheatfields. The tall, shimmering, golden wheat swayed with the tiniest breeze, and, depending on the direction of its movement, it would expose or hide the objects of our search, huge orange poppies and sky-blue cornflowers. The wheat was much taller than any one of us; we played hide-and-seek, picked wildflowers, and chased butterflies. At times we scared ourselves silly by pretending to be lost forever in this shimmering jungle. Before we knew it, our mothers were calling us; it was time to go home.

I wasn't always playing with my cousins and friends. There were quiet times curled up with an exciting book, playing checkers and dominoes with my father, or, on Saturday mornings, sitting quietly with my parents and listening to the hour-long classical-music radio program of symphonies or operas.

By far my favorite way to spend time was to do things with my father. During the long, cold, winter nights he built all sorts of magical things for me. A miniature carousel that he designed and built with all movable parts had hand-carved horses and other animals that went up and down, twinkling lights that shone like stars, and even a music box. I helped to paint every inch of it. This project took us most of the winter of 1937–38. But nothing could beat the excitement of riding off to the countryside on warm summer days, sitting on the luggage rack of his motorcycle and holding on to his belt, with my braids whipping around in the wind as we bounced on rough country roads. Bumpity-bump, up and down hills on narrow lanes between trees dappled by early-morning sun, I would squeal with delight and the sheer joy of being alive.

Our destination was usually a visit to the overseer of our timberland, a vast and incredibly beautiful forested area interspersed with meadows dotted with bright wildflowers. In the midst of this nature wonderland was a farmhouse occupied by the overseer and his family. We were always warmly welcomed and immediately invited into the house and served a huge farm breakfast—home-cured ham, scrambled eggs with

With my father and his motorcycle in the summer of 1939.

wild mushrooms, and home-baked bread with jam and freshly churned butter, all usually accompanied by bowls of just-picked wild strawberries with pure cream. We always left home before breakfast, and after our long ride from town I was famished and could hardly wait for this bountiful meal. Some memories never fade.

In retrospect, it was a very simple village life. No indoor plumbing—water was fetched from the well, and we had to use chamber pots or the outhouse. There were no stores selling ready-to-wear clothing. Mother had a seamstress who came every few months, and we designed all my clothes, with her usually spending a week or so sewing all the creations, including underwear; my parents' clothes were also custom made. And we had a shoemaker; he did an outline of my feet and all my shoes fit perfectly. There was laundry time, when two or three washerwomen came to the house for a few days of total chaos with presoaking tubs, scrub-boards, and so on. When all the cleaning and rinsing was accomplished they would hang the laundry in the attic. Then, after it dried, the women ironed and folded each piece and the house would be back in order till the next time, usually two or three months away. The attic also served as a winter storage place for apples and pears. We had a cellar for storing many root vegetables, barrels of home-made sauerkraut, pickled beets, and crocks full of cherry wine, loaded with the aforementioned cherries. I remember the work-horses pulling wagons full of lumber, the well-trained German shepherd watchdog who had been taught to attack all trespassers, and my little cocker spaniel, "Mushka," who slept with me every night. I remember, too, the shiny, bright red floors in the parlor, covered by oriental carpets; a house always full of my parents' friends; the nights of bridge games, music, and dancing; and, most of all, the joy and laughter.

Then, due to my mother's health problems, we moved to Aleksandrow, Kujawski, in the mid-summer of 1938. My idyllic Radziejow life had come to an end. Now I was going to be a city kid.

If we were to have moved anywhere other than Aleksandrow I would have been heartbroken. But this was different: I loved Aleksandrow. My mother's parents, my beloved Grandma Helenka and Grandpa Zigmund, lived there. Now I wouldn't have to wait for trips—I could see them every day, whenever I wanted to. Not only were my grandparents living there, but also my dad's sister Berta, whose son, Heniek, was my age; we always played together when I went to Aleksandrow. And oh, yes, there was my best friend, Tobia; my cousin Adaś, the son of my mother's cousin Nadzia; and tons of great-aunts and great-uncles, all of them related to my mother. I was a very happy camper. Life was going to be grand!

Even though it was only maybe twenty or thirty miles from Radziejow to Aleksandrow, socially and culturally they were in two different worlds. Radziejow was barely more than a village, while Aleksandrow, though not a large city, was much more cosmopolitan and sophisticated. I would be going to third grade at a real city school. My new teacher had been a school friend of my mother, and it made me feel very important to have a personal connection to my teacher. I was a good student and quickly became the teacher's pet. The curriculum was exciting and demanding. In the third grade we were studying Polish history, geography, geology, and math, as well as art and music. Foreign language was mandatory in the fifth grade for students planning to advance past the eighth grade and continue with their education at the high school. For me that was a given. Everyone in my mother's family had at least a high-school education, and most of her cousins were college graduates.

My father started a lumber-brokerage business. I had no idea what it meant, except that he traveled all around Poland and Eastern Europe to buy and sell carloads of lumber. He was gone for a week or two at a time, and I missed him. No more evenings of fun and games. I was growing up and life was changing. Now, instead of playing games with Daddy, I played Chinese checkers with a new girl friend. We had tea parties for our dolls and became inseparable; she was my new best friend. Despite school and my busy social life I always found time to visit my beloved grandparents.

We lived in a brand-new, modern apartment building. Each unit had its own large balcony adorned with baskets of trailing petunias cascading over the railing. Of course this was in the summer, when we moved in; nothing grew during the cold, harsh, winter months, when the balcony was covered with ice and snow. As time went by, I made new friends in my neighborhood and hardly ever saw my boy cousins or my old girl friend Tobia. The days of our make-believe tea parties at Grandma's home were over. Now I was more interested in board games and reading books.

I was still a tomboy at heart, and during that cold winter I managed to get myself into all kinds of daredevil troubles. One particular incident stands out in my memory. I was wearing a brand-new coat when one of the boys dared me to mount my sled on my belly and slide down an icy hill. Having done this numerous times in my life I agreed, never taking into consideration the barbed-wire fence at the bottom of this very steep hill. Well, I made it, but my poor coat got hung up on the barbed wire and badly torn. I concocted some kind of sad story and my mother believed me. Most of the time, though, I was a really good kid, and hardly ever needed discipline.

Even though I was enjoying life in Aleksandrow, there was a tension in the air. The adults seemed awfully preoccupied, and everyone was talking about Germany. There was also a lot of excitement in our home. I was very ill with scarlet fever. Mother and I were quarantined in our apartment for six weeks — she couldn't leave, and no one was permitted to enter. She nursed me around the clock. Grandma and Grandpa brought us food and left it outside the door. Daddy had been away when I got sick and he couldn't come in if he wanted to continue to work. I remember a terribly sore throat and very high fever; whenever I woke up, Mother was sponging me with cold water. Eventually I became more coherent and

With my parents, Aleksandrow, 1938.

could swallow some water or juice. I spent a couple of weeks in bed peeling my skin, which I had to put into envelopes that were then sealed and burned. After I recovered, I learned that the disease had been epidemic at my school and one of my classmates had died.

I was barely back in school when I was informed that my favorite uncle—Uncle Moniek, my mother's only sibling—was leaving for America. It had taken years for him to get papers to emigrate to Portland, Oregon, to marry his American sweetheart, Hanita Asher. They had met in 1934 when she and her mother were on a grand European tour. Hanita and her mother were traveling all over Poland, meeting her mother's relatives. It seems that they were related to my great-grandmother, and one of their stops was Aleksandrow, where Moniek and Hanita met at a family gathering. This was one of those storybook romances. They met; she spoke only English; he spoke Polish, German, French, Yiddish, and not a word of English; but somehow during that twenty-four-hour visit they fell in love. Carrying flowers and chocolates, he went to see her off at the train station. They waved goodbye, and she was gone. But this goodbye was actually the beginning of a long-distance romance. They corresponded for the four years it took her to get him out of Poland. At last, in November 1938, the whole family—except for me, still recovering from scarlet fever—escorted him to the train station. My father accompanied Moniek to Gdynia, the only seaport city in Poland. There Uncle Moniek boarded the ship bound for America, and my father came home. Neither one of them imagined that this was to be their last goodbye.

In the fall of 1938 the abuse of Jews in Germany escalated to unprecedented proportions. Shortly after Moniek left for America, trainloads of German Jews began passing through Aleksandrow. I was too young to comprehend the situation, but I knew that something terrible was happening in Germany. Every few nights Daddy went to the train station and came home with strangers who did not speak Polish. Mother always had

With Uncle Moniek, Aleksandrow, 1937.

a hot meal waiting for them. My parents and the strangers would sit at the table, eating and whispering in a foreign language that I did not understand. Yet I felt a palpable sense of fear and desperation. I wasn't allowed to hang around and would be sent to bed. I tried to stay awake, listening to the whispers through the closed doors, hoping to hear something. Sometimes I heard the women crying. In the mornings when I got up the house would be quiet and our guests would be gone. Eventually I learned that most of these people, business acquaintances or family friends, were from Berlin and Hamburg. My mother's family had close personal ties to many Jews in Germany, France, and England.

Suddenly it all stopped and life returned to normal. But it wasn't quite normal — something was askew in the looks my parents exchanged, the whispered conversations that ceased when I entered a room.

Eventually I was informed that we were going to live in Australia. Once we were settled there, my parents would get papers to bring my mother's parents there as well, and Uncle Moniek would also be trying to get them to America. In early January of 1939, in the midst of a nasty snowstorm, I went with my parents to an embassy to obtain our Australian passports. Australia needed builders and architects. Father had qualified for the architectural quota, and we were going to emigrate there. All that was left for us to do in order to get out of Poland was to obtain our passports and visas. We had already been approved and all the prerequisites were taken care of.

This was the last step. We stood in a long line of desperate people, impatiently waiting for our turn to enter the embassy, sign some documents, and get our final papers. After many hours we were almost to the entrance, when a man came out and announced that the Jewish quota had been filled for the entire year. He said, blithely, "Come back next year." He had no idea that he had just handed us a death warrant. Our last chance to get out of Poland and Europe had vanished. The next year we were under German occupation, and our fate was sealed.

With all avenues of departure closed to us, my parents did what they thought was the next best thing. Because Aleksandrow was a central hub of Polish railroad transportation, everyone was afraid that if Germany attacked Poland the city could become a target for German air raids to disrupt and destroy Polish trains.

Father went to adjoining small towns searching for a safer place. In the spring of 1939 my parents selected Lubraniec as our next home. Daddy found a lovely large apartment for us and a great location for his new lumberyard. Shortly thereafter he and Mother moved to Lubraniec, leaving me with my grandparents to finish the school year. I joined them in June after finishing the third grade.

Aleksandrow was pivotal in my young life. Even though I actually lived there for barely a year, it holds a special place in my heart. This was the city where from a very early age most of my childhood desires were fulfilled by my grandparents. It was also the starting point for all of our vacations and trips to Ciechocinek, a very popular resort city, and to Torun, an old city dating back to the twelfth century.

My mother used to take me to Ciechocinek for health treatments. Every summer we went for a few weeks and Daddy would come on weekends; Grandpa Zigmund and Uncle Moniek also came very often since it was only a half-hour train ride from Aleksandrow. I remember the mineral health spas and the mineral-water kiosks where one could get many different flavored drinks, all supposedly very good for curing most of mankind's ills. There were concerts in the park, and wonderful restaurants with absolutely the most fabulous chilled cherry soup. Every year we rented the same little place. I made many friends from all over Poland, and all of us looked forward to our annual reunions. In the evenings I stayed in our room with a babysitter while Mother would get all dressed up and leave for the constant whirl of adult evening parties. I could hardly wait for Mother to leave. My teenage babysitters had great imaginations

With my mother and grandparents, Ciechocinek, 1936.

and we had wonderful adventures without ever leaving the room.

Visits to Torun with Mother and Grandpa were also very exciting. Though it is an old city, my memories are of one of the newer sections, with wide boulevards lined by trees, sidewalk cafés, streetcars, beautiful store-window displays, and magnificent living quarters. We always stayed with my mother's uncle and aunt, Adolf and Mala. He was an international attorney, and as was the custom in those days his office was in part of their large apartment, with a separate entrance for his clients. Their residence was on the third floor, and I remember standing in the parlor by the bay window, watching the street below for people arriving and departing in their fancy limousines. That was a sight that a small-town kid just didn't see at home, and I was informed that all those people coming and going were his German clients. Aunt Mala was a socialite: she smoked cigarettes in long holders, played cards, and went out every day. She taught me to play gin rummy and took me to the park and on all kinds of excursions. Their only daughter, Stefka, was my mother's age, and they were very close, almost like sisters. Stefka was a divorcée — quite scandalous — and spent most of her time traveling all around Europe. A couple of years before the war she married David. They settled in Torun in a twelve-room apartment, and their first and only child, Ludwig, was born in 1938.

My parents' concerns about Aleksandrow were well founded. The city would be badly damaged. People left there in droves, and many of them came through Lubraniec, going east, possibly to Russia. We heard their horrific tales of the destruction of Aleksandrow.

RETURN TO SOMPOLNO AND RADZIEJOW

Sompolno had a large and flourishing Jewish population. It vanished in the horrors of Chelmno and the other death camps. Many years after the war, Unkie told me that my paternal grandparents had been very wealthy. Rich or poor, it made no difference to the Nazis. All the Jewish residents from Sompolno were rounded up in the middle of the night and taken to Chelmno. Uncle Icek, his wife, Andzia, and their daughter, Tusia, survived that night. One of his Catholic employees allowed them to hide on his property. They had a five-year-old son and an eleven-year-old daughter. The little boy, Nahum, was a very outgoing and active youngster. His parents were aware that even if he was very good but made one tiny little sound at the wrong time all of their lives would be in jeopardy—including the lives of their benefactors, since if a Polish family was caught hiding even one Jew, that Polish family was always severely punished by the Germans, and often would be murdered. My aunt and uncle made a heartbreaking choice. They opted to leave their son with Grandpa Menahem and Grandma Hinda, and took their daughter with them into hiding. My little cousin went to the Chelmno extermination camp with our grandparents. My aunt and uncle paid a tremendous emotional price to save their daughter.

After the war, Uncle Icek, having survived internment in several concentration camps, went back to Sompolno searching for his wife, family, and friends. He found no one. Not even one Jew had returned to Sompolno. The locals were not welcoming and in fact were extremely hostile. He was afraid to remain there for an extended period of time, but he and his wife had agreed to meet in Sompolno if they survived. Despite his fear, he went to many places asking if anyone had seen his wife or any other member of his family. Finally he learned that a few weeks prior to his arrival his wife had come to Sompolno looking for him. She was afraid to stay and left town after a few hours. Once he got that information he left Sompolno. Miraculously, not only did he find his wife, Andzia, but, to his great joy and amazement, his daughter, Tusia, had also survived the Holocaust. They lived in Poland for a few years and then emigrated to Israel shortly after it became a country. My uncle, who before the war had owned a brick factory in Sompolno with more than a hundred employees, became an English teacher, first in Poland and then in Israel. He was fluent in numerous languages and a member of the Esperanto movement, with which he became involved as a student at a Belgian university.

Uncle Icek was an exceptional man. When he heard of my forthcoming trip to Poland, he wistfully asked me to visit Sompolno. He wanted to know how it looked fifty-plus years after the Holocaust. He was also interested in the people who lived there. Did they remember the Jewish families who were once an integral part of Sompolno's social and economic structure? I promised him that I would go there and upon my return give him a detailed report of my impressions.

In retrospect, the visit to Sompolno was very pleasant. All the locals gawked at the tour bus of Americans parked in their village square. It is a pretty little town, clean and well maintained. Our guide, Wloclaw, assisted me with English–Polish translation. We met a woman whose father had worked for my grandfather. She remembered the Kominkowski name and the lumber mill, and though she had been quite young and didn't remember much else, she said that the Kominkowski family had been very nice and good to work for. She admitted to her family's hiding a couple of Jews, but they were not from my family. After a few more questions and answers she seemed ill at ease, and bade us a quick goodbye and walked away. Shortly thereafter, as *we were walking, a young man came up behind me and planted a tender kiss on my cheek. He ran away, smiling and waving. Why did he pick me out of our group? We never exchanged a word but it felt good—like a welcoming back, a feeling of "I like seeing you here."*

A young woman came up to us at the opposite end of the town square. She was eager to assist me in my quest for information related to the Jewish residents of Sompolno. In the short time we had spent walking around with me asking questions, word had spread throughout the community. This younger woman had no personal knowledge, but she was sure that her elderly mother remembered many things. She asked us to wait while she fetched her mother. Soon she returned with a tiny, wrinkled old lady who immediately engaged in an animated conversation with Wloclaw. She remembered many things and names, including members of my family, but had no idea of what had happened to them. She also remembered the lumber mill, which had burned down many years ago. How sad that even our mill was destroyed.

The woman and her daughter proudly told us about the synagogue down the street. The Sompolno community had completely restored it, and it now houses the local library. They were very proud of this achievement. I had the feeling that this was the town's monument to their murdered Jews. We headed for the library-synagogue, walking along a narrow cobbled street flanked on either side by old adjoining houses whose front doors opened directly onto the broken-down sidewalk. Within a few minutes we spotted the synagogue. It was by far the largest and most impressive building on that particularly impoverished-looking side street. I believe that the exterior appearance had not been changed. It looked like a well-maintained Polish small-town Shul, with a prominent star of David over the entrance welcoming its congregants for a daily minyan or the Sabbath service, but instead we found ourselves entering a fairly modern library. The librarian welcomed us and pulled out archives of old newspaper articles, carefully displayed in an album about the Jews of Sompolno. She seemed genuinely

pleased to meet us and proudly shared this important historical informa-
tion with our group. Glancing through it, I saw nothing relating to my fam-
ily. It seemed as though none of us had ever existed, even though the family
had lived there for so many generations.

I was very fortunate to have met up with the women before going to
the library. They were a link to the past, and thus gave me a reaffirmation
of self and the sense of connection with my murdered family. My relatives
had worshipped in that synagogue and I am pleased that it is still standing
and maintained in excellent condition. Its use as a library seems very ap-
propriate, not at all a desecration—a synagogue has always been meant to
be a place of study and learning as well as a house of prayer. There are no
more Jews in Sompolno. Let the library be a place of enlightenment.

As we boarded our bus I was acutely aware of being a link between
the past and the future, and of feeling a bond with the many generations of
my father's family who had lived, loved, and died in that little Polish town.
My promise to Uncle Icek was fulfilled. In all probability I am the last mem-
ber of the Kominkowski family ever to set foot in Sompolno, Poland.

Twelve years earlier, in 1986, I took a cruise to Mexico, where, for the first
time since coming to America, I met other Polish Jewish Holocaust survi-
vors. One man in the group proceeded to question me as to where I had
lived in Poland. I replied, "Łodz ghetto," and he impatiently said, "No, not
the ghetto, where did you live before the war? What town?" When I men-
tioned Sompolno and Radziejow, he became very agitated and impatient.
"Which Radziejow?" "Kujawski," I replied. "What was your last name?" As
I told him, all color drained from his face. He looked me in the eye and said,
"Your family had the lumberyard down in the valley. I lived in the town up
on the hill. I knew your family. For forty years I have been searching for sur-
vivors from our region and you are the first and only one that I have met!"

I was stunned by his statement. In this unbelievable cruise-ship set-
ting, in the middle of the Pacific Ocean, I had just met a man who knew

my family. He knew my aunts and uncles; he could tell me what happened to Lydzia and Jusiek. I could barely breathe. Slowly I regained some semblance of composure and started asking him questions about my family. Instantly his wife interfered and would not permit me to continue on the subject. Later on she told me about her husband's severe heart condition, that she was terrified that our conversation could bring on another heart attack. For a number of years I had suspected that there were not many survivors from my region of Poland. Could it be possible that just myself, my aunt, uncle, and cousin, and this one man were the only survivors from the Kujawski region of Poland? I hope and pray that there were a few more. For sure there were five of us. Five out of several hundred thousand!

After our friendly reception in Sompolno I could hardly wait to visit Radziejow. I was full of anticipation. Sixty years earlier, when we moved to Aleksandrow, my parents had taken me from this place of magic dreams and make-believe life. Returning after all this time, would I be able to recognize some of the place? Would the lumberyard still exist? What about the steep lane by our house leading to the top of the hill? Would I find the town square up there or had it all changed? All these questions silently running around and around in my head. . . . Well, I would just have to wait and see.

We were now approaching the outskirts of town, driving past familiar-looking fields and farmlands. It was difficult to contain my excitement. Our bus was climbing up a steep hill in a circular fashion, no sign of a lane going straight up. We were on a well-paved road, dotted with houses, winding its way around and around to the top of the hill. The road was narrow and our bus driver could barely manage to make the sharp turns. At last one final steep curve and there it was—the village square. Surrounded by ramparts, it perched on top of the hill. My excitement mounted: yes, my memories had validity. Unfortunately, a few minutes after our arrival, the church bells began ringing. The local residents had no time to stop and chat with us. They were rushing to church for the evening vespers. We walked around the ramparts. I looked down to the flat land below, hoping to spot the lane or maybe even get a glimpse of the lumberyard, but unfortunately after all those years nothing looked the same. At last an older man walked past us and our guide asked him about the location of the lumberyard. The man answered, "Oh, that was on the opposite side of town, over there down the hill, but you won't find it, since the yard burned down many years ago."

After that conversation we meandered aimlessly around the square. Right smack in the center of it I noticed some statuary, which upon closer examination turned out to be a lovely memorial to Radziejow's World War II victims. I believe that it included their Jewish residents.

There was no reason to linger in Radziejow. There was nothing and no one there for me, just the glimmering ghosts of my childhood. We boarded our bus and departed.

By a strange coincidence, both the lumber mill in Sompolno and our lumberyard in Radziejow were totally destroyed by fire. The owners of these businesses—my grandparents, parents, aunts, and uncles—and all of their descendants, with the exception of myself, Uncle Icek, Aunt Andzia, and my cousin Tusia, were murdered in the infernos of Auschwitz, Chelmno, and Treblinka. The word "Holocaust" means destruction by fire. In the case of my family, fire consumed even the physical evidence of our existence in those two Polish towns.

Chapter Two

LUBRANIEC

1939–1941

My parents moved to Lubraniec in the spring of 1939, while I remained in Aleksandrow with my grandparents. In June, following the end of the school year, I was reunited with my parents. Lubraniec was a cultural shock, since we had no friends or close family there. Although there were some cousins of my parents, this didn't help much since none of them had kids my age. We lived in a very nice apartment with spacious rooms, but it was hard to be enthusiastic about that when I had no friends and no one to play with.

When finally I did meet some local kids, they were extremely uneasy around me. They were from poverty-stricken circumstances, while I was from another world. They lived with their whole families — parents, grandparents, siblings — in one-room shacks attached to each other along narrow alleyways; it made no difference whether they were Catholics or Jews. Compared to them I had so much, a whole room all to myself, full of dolls, games, toys, and lots of books — and it took a few weeks for us to be comfortable with each other. After a while, when they let me join them and play prison ball, they found that I was a powerful catcher and that broke the ice. At last I had some friends!

I had assumed that Mother and I would be going on our annual trip to Ciechocinek, but to my surprise there was a change in plans and I was told that I would be going to Torun to visit Stefka, David, and baby Ludwig. It would be a two-week vacation, and Mother would join me for the second week. I was so excited about this adventure that I could hardly wait for my departure, but at last it was time to go. There were just a few weeks left before the beginning of the school year. This trip was far and beyond anything I had ever experienced. Luxuriating in the splendor of their huge home, with a cook, maid, and nanny—and the most impressive indoor bathrooms with hot and cold running water, real toilet paper, and bathtubs—was so far removed from my simple small-town life that it felt surreal.

On about the fourth or fifth day of my visit, Stefka had a phone call from my mother. As soon as she hung up I was informed that Mother wasn't coming, and that I had to go home. The maid packed my bag and Stefka took me to the train station. She was very upset and said something about Germany attacking Poland and that I needed to be home with my parents. When we arrived at the station, throngs of people were milling around and everyone was determined to board a train. It seemed to make no difference to anyone which train they got on as long as it went someplace else away from our part of the country, which was fairly close to the German border. Stefka spoke to the conductor and found me a seat. The conductor promised her that he would look after me and get me off in Aleksandrow. Grandpa Zigmund would be there to meet me.

Feeling terribly alone and quite insecure, I sat quietly by a window and watched the passing landscape. The conductor announced, "Next stop, Aleksandrow," and before he had a chance to get me I was out of my seat and on my way to the door. Grandpa was waiting for me and I was so happy to see him. Giving me a big bear hug, he said that there was not much time for us to get to the bus depot. We had to hurry to get there in time for me to board the bus for Lubraniec, and there would be no time to see Grandma Helenka. Huffing and puffing, we made it in time. Grandpa managed to find me a seat on the crowded bus, then kissed me goodbye and left. The trip home was very scary. People were pushing and shoving; with every seat occupied they were standing in the aisle trying not to fall on the seated passengers as the bus bounced up and down on the poorly paved country road. At last we arrived in Lubraniec, and I was home.

The next day I realized that nothing was the same. At the end of our lane was a potato field, but instead of potato pickers there were men furiously digging trenches. Intended for use as air-raid shelters, the trenches were dug in a zigzag pattern in an attempt to save the most lives. Germany had attacked Poland, and without any formal notice we were at war! We had absolutely no anti-aircraft defenses, and the German pilots flew low, strafing farmers as they were working in the fields, enjoying killing innocent civilians. This lasted for a few days, with air-raid sirens blaring and everyone running to the ditches, trying to hide in them and hoping to be invisible. On the day they began to really bomb our town it was already occupied by the German army. The German soldiers quickly spread swastika flags on top of their tanks and the bombing stopped.

One memory that stands out from that period of time is the retreating Polish cavalry. Needing materials to build a temporary bridge over the river, they purchased lumber from our yard and paid my father with a note promising payment in Polish currency. Once they had crossed the river they blew up the bridge to slow down the German pursuit. The entire process took maybe two or three hours. Later that same day, the German tanks arrived, and they took more lumber to rebuild the bridge and chase the retreating Polish soldiers. The Germans, though, did not pay or give a promissory note—they just helped themselves. And that was a small preview of our future under the Nazi regime.

Lubraniec was occupied by the Germans without resistance. The local citizens lined the sidewalks to greet the conquering troops, hoping to get better treatment in return for their welcoming gesture. Of course this proved to be a delusion.

From the beginning of the German invasion, a constant caravan of horse-drawn carts, loaded with household possessions and with children perched on top of the piles, wound its way through our little town. Everyone was running away from the Germans. Many were going to eastern

Poland and Russia; some were just on the move without any clear idea of their destination. Among the first to arrive were Grandma Helenka and Grandpa Zigmund. They had come to live with us. We gave them my bedroom and I moved in with my parents. Shortly thereafter, Uncle Adolf and Aunt Mala arrived from Torun with Stefka, David, and Ludwig. They also moved in with us. Lubraniec was overflowing with refugees and there were no available rentals. What had been a spacious home for the three of us and passable for five had suddenly been transformed into a congested rooming house. I don't remember any complaints, though, but rather the feeling that it was good for the family to be together. Somehow we managed.

My father had been right to bring us out of Aleksandrow. The city was pretty much destroyed, and our apartment building was firebombed and went up in flames. My grandparents' home had received a direct bomb hit and was razed to the ground; by deciding to join us in Lubraniec they had gotten out in the nick of time. Most of our friends and relatives from Aleksandrow had lost their homes, and many of them came through Lubraniec on the way east. The retreating Polish army had confiscated a great many horses, and those not lucky enough to hang onto theirs had no choice but to harness up and pull their wagons themselves.

Many of those friends and relatives begged my parents to join them. One night I overheard my mother and father arguing. They thought that I was asleep and I never let on that I was listening to every word. Daddy was pleading with Mother: "Ruta, please! We need to go. We need to save ourselves and our child. We have to save Marychna, we have to leave!" Mother said, "No! I won't go!" Father continued, "I'm begging you. We should not stay here, let's go. I am willing to leave my parents and siblings behind. We can ask your parents to join us, but if they don't want to go we have to leave without them." Mother was adamant that she would not leave her parents. "Besides," she argued, "nothing will happen to us. We are Polish nationals first and Jews second." Even though she had hosted all those forcibly displaced German Jews, she stuck to her upper-middle-class outlook. *It can happen to them, but not to us.* Mother refused to leave her parents, and Grandma in turn refused to leave her brother, Adolf, who had recently suffered a massive heart attack and was in no condition to travel. That was the end of that subject. We remained in Lubraniec. Uncle Adolf died two weeks later, but by then it was impossible to leave. The noose had tightened around the Jewish population of Lubraniec, as it had around all the Jews in Poland.

Change came quickly. Within hours after the German occupation of Lubraniec the Jewish residents lost all legal and human rights. School started a week late, but unfortunately I could not be among the students. *Goodbye, fourth grade. This is not for me anymore. I am a Jew and therefore forbidden to have any kind of education, either public or private.* While all of my Catholic playmates went back to school, I stayed indoors at home, read books or drew pictures, and played with Ludwig. After school hours I was allowed to go out and play with my friends. It was much safer outside when non-Jewish children were also playing there. As a group we never attracted German curiosity and they left us alone. As a solitary child during school hours I would have been much more noticeable and possibly identified as a Jew, which could have led to a beating or other abuse by a member of the SS or any German soldier.

We lived in constant fear. I remember the notices posted on buildings, the blaring announcements amplified by megaphones from moving vehicles. Some were for the general population regarding curfew or other constraints, but most of them were directed at Jews. We had to wear two yellow stars on the outside of our garments, one on the front, on the right side of the chest, and the other one on the back of the left shoulder. At all times these must be prominently visible. Jews, considered subhuman by the Germans, were not permitted to walk on the sidewalks; instead we were to walk in the middle of the road with the other animals, which were mostly horses since horse and buggy was the typical mode of transportation in our region. Jews were issued ration cards for food, with our allotted portions barely a notch above a starvation diet. We were not permitted to buy meat, eggs, or dairy, except for the tiny bit allowed on our ration cards.

The German soldiers never knocked. Lords and masters, they marched right into our homes as if they owned them. Our second-floor apartment had a private entrance. One day we heard soldiers storming up the stairs. Yelling obscenities, they entered the kitchen, as we, terrified by their noise, stood there waiting to see what it was that they wanted from us. Within seconds one of them, obviously the commander of this little group, was screaming in German, "Where is it? What did you do with it? Where did you hide it? Where is that barrel of sauerkraut? You swine, you'll pay for this crime!" We felt totally helpless, having no idea what they were talking about. Two of them headed for the parlor and back bedroom, hunting for the stolen sauerkraut. We were afraid to laugh but it was really comical: grown men crawling around the rooms looking in the cupboards and under the tables and beds for a barrel of sauerkraut. The leader was searching the kitchen when suddenly he saw another door, and he pointed at it, screaming, "What are you hiding behind that door?" Stefka gave him a withering look and calmly said, "Please lower your voice. It's a bedroom. My little boy is taking a nap in there." He pushed Stefka ahead of him through the door, Mother and I following them as ordered. Entering the room, he saw the crib, and walked over to it to look down at the sleeping child. Instantly his whole demeanor changed. Softly, he whispered, "What is his name?" "Ludwig," was the reply. He bent over and gently stroked the little blond head. (Ludwig, like his mother, was a blue-eyed blonde.) Time stood still as we watched the transformation of this vicious brute into a regular human being. Finally he whispered, "My son is about the same age. His name is also Ludwig, and there is a great resemblance between our two children." On the verge of tears, he silently beckoned us to follow him and tiptoed out of the bedroom. Back in the kitchen he looked around and way up high on a shelf he spotted a stash of homemade soap. Speaking in a perfectly cultivated voice he advised Mother and Stefka to hide the soap in a more discreet place. He informed them that the soap was a forbidden item and he wouldn't want anyone to confiscate it from us. He bowed deeply to the ladies and clicked his heels, then collected his cohorts and left. After all, they were on a mission, looking for the stolen sauerkraut. I imagine that by the time they arrived at the next house he had composed himself and reverted to his normal behavior.

Shortly after that incident, David, who had written many letters to his family with no response, decided that he had to find them. He and Stefka knew that Jews were not permitted to travel, but they felt that they had to take the chance. They would not wear the yellow stars, and planned to blend in with the gentile population. Accompanied by Ludwig and Aunt Mala, and traveling light with a single small suitcase, they left Lubraniec for Galicia, the area of Poland where David's family lived. Anxiously we waited to hear from them, but we never did. Stefka, David, Ludwig, and Aunt Mala vanished into the void that became the Holocaust.

The living conditions and quality of life continued to deteriorate for the Jews of Lubraniec. Jewish businesses were confiscated. It became very dangerous for Jewish men to walk on the streets, particularly the elderly or bearded — and the more devout, who wore skull caps. German soldiers constantly forced these men into menial slave labor. One of the more degrading jobs they had to perform was sweeping horse manure from the cobbled streets into large buckets; they then had to carry the filled buckets to the fields on the outskirts of town, empty them, and return. Since everyone in the countryside traveled by horse and buggy in the summer — or, in the winter, horse and sleigh — this was a never-ending job, repeated over and over, every day. Even worse, the men were forced to clean human fecal waste from the outhouses; and, as though this was not foul enough, they were often forced to go down into the pit and shovel excrement into a container and then pass it up over their heads. The German soldiers and the SS supervised the toiling Jews, forcing them to work at these awful tasks for eight to ten hours without a break for food, drink, or bathroom. Pushed beyond endurance, they were brutally beaten if they faltered or fell. Sometimes they were beaten for no reason, the soldiers torturing the old Jews just for the fun of it.

One time Grandpa went out on an errand and did not come back until late at night. We didn't dare to go looking for him; that would have been dangerous and could have put another family member in jeopardy. As hard as it was, we sat at home, hoping and praying for his safe return. When he finally came home, he was covered with mud and dried blood, and reeked of horse manure. He had been beaten for some unknowable offense, and forced into horse-manure duty. We were thrilled that he was alive and not injured, but "just" beaten up. And this was nothing out of the ordinary; such incidents happened to most of the Jewish families in our town.

All Jews, including children, had to wear the yellow stars. But from the beginning my parents decided that, because I had the advantage of not looking Jewish, I would be much safer without them. It was still very dangerous, but they believed that I would have a better chance of survival if I blended in with the general population. They must have been right, since I walked freely on the sidewalks with anonymity, and was never challenged. My long, straight, chestnut hair, usually braided, and my fairly small, straight nose did not appear "Jewish" to the German occupiers. Jews had been put on meager rations of food and clothing, and not wearing the yellow stars meant that I could go to places to buy meat and dairy products that the local gentiles were forbidden to sell to Jews. Thus, before I saw my tenth birthday, I had become the chief procurer of forbidden foods for our household. The butcher knew my parents, and friendly neighbors down the street who had a small farm provided me with eggs and milk. My not wearing the Jewish stars gave them a little more protection in that they could deny any knowledge of my identity, but, even so, they were taking a big chance and putting themselves in danger in order to help us.

We had neighbors who were of German descent. Until the occupation they were part of the community; they spoke Polish and there was really no distinction between them and the rest of us. Once Germany occupied our town, though, they became very important, and were treated with great respect by the invaders. One such family lived next door to us. The man owned a business and was friendly with my father. When our radios were confiscated, this neighbor placed his radio close to an open side window. Daddy hid in the bushes and listened to the German newscasts, then translated the news into Polish for our neighbors, who themselves neither understood nor spoke German. Unlike many Polish Germans, this family was not enamored of either Hitler or the Third Reich. They had a daughter who was my age; we had played together before the occupation and continued to do so after it was forbidden for local Germans to fraternize with Jews. One day while we were playing in their home there was an unexpected visitor. The chief SS officer was knocking on the door. The mother gave us a look, saying, "Act natural and continue to play with your dolls," then opened the door and cheerfully welcomed him. He entered, gave us a big grin, and engaged in conversation with the adults for a few minutes, and then left. Shortly thereafter, when it appeared safe, I went home.

Maybe a week or two after that incident, while walking on the sidewalk and carrying an illicit dead chicken in a basket carelessly slung over my arm, I encountered the same SS man. Fear gripped me as he walked toward me. *How should I behave? What do I do?* Hope sprang up as I thought that maybe he wouldn't recognize me and we would just pass each other. No such luck: within seconds we were a few feet apart. He smiled at me and raised his arm in a "Heil Hitler!" salute. My heart racing with fear, I forced myself to smile and return his salute. As we passed each other I carefully kept the same easy pace, and thanked my lucky stars that I had encountered him after the chicken had been butchered and couldn't cluck. Thoughts were running helter-skelter through my head: *What if he had encountered me on the way to the kosher butcher, and the chicken had clucked? What if he got nosy and wanted to know what I was doing?* He would have figured out that I was a Jewish kid walking on the forbidden sidewalk with an illegally acquired chicken. *What if, what if, what if?* A million scenarios were milling around in my head. So many people could have been killed or severely punished: my parents, my grandparents, the people who sold us the chicken, and even the German neighbors for associating with Jews. This incident ended my career of acquiring food for the family. My mother said, "It is just too dangerous!"

My father's lumberyard had been closed since the occupation, and by the fall of 1939 the Germans were confiscating many Polish-owned businesses. Private German citizens were arriving in droves and taking whatever store appealed to them. Since most stores had adjoining living quarters, the owners had to vacate their homes as well as their businesses.

A prominent Polish Catholic family was given half of our apartment. An SS officer came to our place and informed my parents that we could keep two rooms, either the kitchen and the back bedroom or the parlor and the other bedroom. We kept the parlor side since it had quite a bit more space than the kitchen option and we needed every inch of space to house the five of us. The new neighbors had to accept what was offered to them. I really can't remember anything about them. I know that there were no children living with them. We had separate entrances, with them going in through the kitchen and us entering from a large patio directly into the parlor.

It seems strange and a bit pretentious to use the term "parlor," but I don't know what else to call this large, multi-use room. Prior to the

German occupation of Lubraniec, the parlor was our social center. There were many pieces of furniture, and I remember in particular the beautiful, round, black teakwood dining table and its many matching upholstered chairs. During my younger years in Radziejow it was my favorite hiding place, since four or five kids could easily fit beneath it.

Before the war my parents had led a very social life. Often their friends came for evenings of supper, bridge, poker, singing, and dancing. If the visitors were family I would be allowed to play gin rummy with them. Aunt Mala from Torun had taught me the game when I was only six or seven years old.

Even before we had to give up half of our home, some of the furniture and many personal items had been sold off or bartered for fuel or food. The Jewish family who lived on the floor below us had a small, home-operated, oil-processing business. Barely eking out a living, they lived in one room behind the oil press. Then the scarcity of fats such as butter and lard created a great demand for cooking oil; the oil suddenly became quite expensive and our neighbors got very rich. During the worst of times, despite all the misery, funny things do happen. The time had come for my parents to sell off another object — Mother's black, seal-fur coat! Jews were forbidden by law to wear furs, so there was absolutely no good reason to hold on to it when it could buy us food and heat. Father also had a full-length, mink-lined, wool coat, to ward off the freezing winter cold. Our newly rich Jewish neighbors coveted both my parents' fur coats, and bought them from us. It seemed to give them great pleasure to possess such finery, although, since they couldn't wear the coats, they hid them inside a down comforter. This family, unlike most of the other Jews in Lubraniec, was well treated by the Germans, and I imagine that they expected not only to survive but to prosper under German occupation, and thought that eventually they would be able to wear the coats. They never got their wish. The fur coats were left in Lubraniec along with all their possessions. They had been lulled into a false sense of security, and in the end were treated just like all the rest of the Jews in town.

By the time we had to live in two rooms, the parlor was almost empty. Most of the living-room furniture, as well as the dining-room set, was either sold or bartered for food. Winter weather was upon us, and as the temperature dropped it was impossible to heat the two rooms. We had barely enough wood to cook our meals, with none left for the heaters. Rising from floor to ceiling, usually against an outside wall, the room heaters were faced with elegant ceramic tiles. Behind their elaborate iron doors was a fireplace, which, stoked with fuel, produced many hours of heat. By the end of 1939, though, we had only enough wood to cook with. The lovely heaters stood as a cold reminder of our plight.

My mother, the lady who earlier had needed to move from Radziejow because she wasn't well enough to climb the steep hill into town — the same woman who had maids, seamstresses, washerwomen, and other people who catered to her desires — underwent an incredible transformation. She held us together, no task too big or too difficult, and she did it all with the most amazing sense of humor. She made everything into an adventure or something to joke about, and, in the privacy of our home, laughter became the secret sword that the SS couldn't take away. It was an intangible possession. No matter how many times the Germans entered our home with their yelling and bullying, after they left she always had a funny comment that would make me squeal with laughter. I realize now that much of the joking and bravado was for my benefit, and I am forever thankful that my parents had the wisdom to teach me how to face adversity and overcome it. They taught me that, no matter what happened, life was to be lived joyously to its fullest potential.

One cold winter morning, Mother calmly announced that the bedroom was turning into an ice cave and that we were moving out of the bedroom into the parlor with Grandma and Grandpa. She did an incredible job. This one room was divided into sections: we had a kitchen area with a table, and cupboards that separated the kitchen from the sleeping and sitting area. She even managed to place the beds lengthwise, with the tall headboards backed up against each other. I slept with my parents in one bed and my grandparents had the other. This furniture placement gave each "bedroom" a sense of privacy. We were quite cozy and also much warmer. The back bedroom was closed off and towels were stuffed around the door to keep out the cold air. By the following summer we had lost interest in the other room, and ended up leaving it vacant.

One day Daddy took me to our dirt cellar, which had been dug way down under the floor of our storage shed. After checking that no one had followed us, he shut and locked the shed door. Once he was certain that we were alone, he opened the trap door and we descended into the cellar. Wielding a flashlight, he showed me four freshly dug holes, one in each corner. I was told to memorize their locations. If we were ever separated I was to come back to Lubraniec after the war. We were all going to meet there, but in the event that they did not return, I should dig up our buried treasures — crystal, pieces of sterling silver, and family jewelry — which would be the basis on which to begin a new life. On another occasion, in a neighbor's barn, we went through a similar procedure. Jews were ordered to turn over all valuable items to the Germans, but many, including my parents, hid what they could, hoping to start anew when the war was over.

In 1940 we had hope that the war might end in the near future. We were still living in our own home, albeit in just one room. We were abused, persecuted, beaten, and deprived of sufficient food to sustain our bodies, but the only thing that mattered was our good health and being together. We heard rumors about labor camps, total starvation, ghettoes, concentration camps, and the separation of families. Despite this awareness, no one among us could foresee what was to come. The civilized mind could not possibly conjure up the vision of extermination camps, with gas chambers and crematoria, created for the sole purpose of mass murder. The names of Auschwitz, Treblinka, Chelmno, Majdanek,

Sobibor, and Belzec — the Nazis' six killing camps, all in Poland — were not yet familiar to us. At that time the most dreaded word was "Dachau" — the name of the first concentration camp established by the Nazis, in southern Germany — and indeed many of our town leaders, the educated intelligentsia, had been deported to Dachau. We didn't know that Hitler's ultimate goal was to murder every Jew in Europe. And so, in the spring of 1940, we buried our family treasures, to be recovered after Germany had lost the war and our lives returned to normal.

I made a new best friend, the girl next door, who had moved with her parents from Torun. I was thrilled to have a playmate from that magical city, but, unhappily for both of us, when her parents learned that I was Jewish she was at first forbidden to play with me. I don't know what changed their minds, but eventually she was allowed to come to my house. We became inseparable. After a year or so, her father became the gatekeeper of a former country estate that had been confiscated from a Polish nobleman for use by the SS as their personal residence. But even after their move to the countryside we continued to be best friends. Her father would drive her into town to spend the day with me, or he would pick me up and take me back to their home.

Whenever I went with him to the country estate, she and I would spend the day sleighing down the icy hills with no other human being in sight and a feeling of complete freedom. This continued throughout the winter of 1940–41; whenever I think of her I see the majestic trees with branches laden with fresh white snow, and the two of us flying down hills on our sleds. I know that there must have been a spring, but of that I have no memories nor any mental images.

As close as we were, I had one secret that couldn't be shared with anyone, including her. I had a tutor! This was such a dangerous act of defiance — all Poles were by now forbidden to pursue education of any kind — that I couldn't share it, even with her. Too many lives were at stake. If the

Germans were to find out they would punish everyone involved: me, my parents, my grandparents, the tutor, the tutor's family, and anyone else who might possibly have known about it.

My education was minimal. Two or three times a week a young Jewish man — I was told that he was a cousin of some sort — would arrive at our apartment to play chess with my father. A table was set by the parlor window, and the two of them, both excellent chess players, were always in the midst of a very competitive game. During the game the young man would get up and come over to the kitchen table, give me an assignment, and return for the next chess move. Father, the watchdog, never left his seat, always on the lookout for an unexpected visitor. If anyone were to come to the apartment I would appear totally involved in my favorite pastime at a table strewn with my drawings and paper and paints. Underneath the litter of art materials were my instructions and my written papers. The young man, a 1939 university graduate with a degree in English, was teaching me English, math, geography, and writing. English was the most important subject because Uncle Moniek had filed papers to bring me and my grandparents to America, and everyone was still hoping that we would be able to leave Poland once we received the papers. That was not to be. My educational routine lasted for a few months during the fall, winter, and spring, and ended in June 1941 when all the able-bodied Jewish men of Lubraniec were shipped off to a slave-labor camp.

During that spring, a few weeks before they took my father away and my world turned upside down, we were invited to an Easter dinner by the local stationmaster, a friend of Daddy's, who lived with his wife and children on a farm a few miles out of town. He must have come to get us; I remember riding in a horse-drawn buggy, and we certainly did not have one, since ours had been confiscated. Although those details are vague, the memory of the rest of that visit has remained crystal clear. Everyone was all dressed up for the holiday. After a year and a half of meager food rations, we entered a dining room that had a table set for a feast.

I had not seen anything like it since the Germans invaded Poland. A large platter of rabbit paté, a delicacy reserved for special occasions, graced the center of the table. After dinner, I and the other kids were excused to go outside to play, while the grownups remained at the table, deep in what seemed a very serious conversation. As my parents were getting ready to leave, I was informed that I would not be going home with them, and that I would be living with these people until the end of the war. There would be no contact between my parents and myself. This family would raise me as their orphaned niece who had come from another part of Poland to live with them. These wonderful people were willing to jeopardize their lives and safety to help a Jewish friend. The friend's child, however, had other ideas. I refused to stay, crying and hollering and telling them in no uncertain terms that I would run away and cause all kinds of problems. The effect was that I made it impossible for the other family to take the risk. I was eleven years old and had been very sheltered by my parents, and I understood neither the inherent danger of being a Jewish child nor the magnificence of this offer of sanctuary. I won, and my parents and I went home.

Life continued in the manner that we had become conditioned to accept. Jews wore the yellow stars, and we were in constant danger of physical brutality, abuse, and starvation — but, no matter what, we were together.

Throughout all of our travails we were aware of Polish farmers and their families quietly traveling through town. They were being evicted from their land, their farms confiscated and given to the constant influx of German immigrants. For weeks we heard the clippity-clop of horses' hoofs as they pulled wagons filled with families and their personal possessions, on their way to who knows where. Most of them passed through at night, and during the day trainloads of German civilians would arrive to take over the confiscated farms. Many of the Polish farmers were sent to work camps in Germany while their families searched for friends or relatives who were willing to take them in. It was a sad time for all Poles.

Nobody knew who would be the next victim of the Third Reich. Jews and Catholics, we all suffered from degradation and persecution, although doubtless the Jews, classified as subhuman, had it by far the worst. Rumors were circulating of mass executions. We heard stories of Jews in nearby towns being rounded up, taken out into the countryside where they were forced to dig the pits that would be their own mass graves, and then murdered. Who could possibly believe all of these tales? Every so often a man would survive the slaughter and escape, and somehow make it to Lubraniec to warn us. Such men went from town to town, hiding in fields and empty barns, telling their awful tales. They seemed mentally disturbed, not really quite right in their behavior. Poor souls, they had obviously experienced some trauma, but, as everyone said: "Come on, no one in their right mind could believe the things they're telling us."

We were warned, but we could not believe it. And even if we had grasped the truth, it would have made no difference. There was no place for us to go, and nowhere to hide. Most of the Polish people were ambivalent, many overtly anti-Semitic; the majority of those who weren't were too scared to offer assistance, fearing that they would jeopardize their families and put their own lives at risk.

Chapter Three

DEPORTATION

1941

And then it happened: the unspoken fear became real. Suddenly and with no warning, the Germans issued an order for all able-bodied Jewish men to report immediately for a work detail in a field on the outskirts of town. They let it be known that if any man did not report, he and his family would be severely punished. There were no options.

We told ourselves that it was only a work detail. Mother, Grandma, Grandpa, and I walked with Daddy to the field. As we walked we were joined by other Jewish families escorting their loved ones. The sidewalks were empty. I don't recall seeing any of our Christian neighbors — just the Jews, walking in the middle of the road, on their way to the field. On a beautiful, balmy, June morning, without a cloud in the sky, the German soldiers met us and at gunpoint ordered all the men to the center of the meadow. Their families were not allowed to go with them.

Army lorries were parked on the perimeter. As we stood there helplessly, without having been allowed even a goodbye kiss or hug, we watched our men climb into the trucks. The men were very crowded and had to remain in a standing position. As soon as the first truck was filled, the Germans began loading the next one and the one after that, until every one of the men was in a truck. Then they closed all the truck gates, formed a caravan, and drove off.

I remember moving slightly away from the crowd of crying people, even away from my mother and grandparents. I was hugging a huge tree, and the tree and I became as one. Not a single tear escaped from my eyes;

they were dry and burning as my whole being focused only on my father. I did not see or hear anyone else. The world stood still. Why were the birds singing? All those pretty wildflowers in bloom and the sun was still shining. Didn't they know that this was the end of the world? My world! They took my daddy; he was my world! I hugged the tree and stared at the disappearing truck until there was nothing to see.

And then we went home. And waited, and waited, and waited. . . . One day, two days, three days. *They went on a work detail; they should be coming home! Well, maybe in a week or two.* Nothing. . . . Then a postcard arrived from a labor camp in Poznań (renamed Posen by the Germans), Camp Radziwill, saying that he was OK. The camp commander seemed to like him, probably because he spoke fluent German and could translate for them. The Germans had wanted to put him in charge of the other prisoners, but somehow or other he managed to get out of it and was working in the infirmary. "Take care of yourselves. I love you." Every so often we received another postcard. No mention ever of camp conditions or of coming home. Just: "I'm OK. Take care of yourselves. I love you, Zalmen." We responded, keeping it just as innocuous, the only kind of correspondence that would pass the German censorship.

After all the able-bodied men were taken from Lubraniec, all that was left of the Jewish population were women, children, the sick, and the elderly. Life became a constant wait for the next postcard from Daddy. Something died in me that day at the meadow. The carefree, adventuresome little girl ceased to exist. From that day in June 1941 till late August, when we were all deported to the Łodz ghetto, the pages in my life are a total blank. Did I play with friends, read books, or just sit at home and mope? I don't know. Vague memories of anxiety, tension, and little knapsacks packed and ready to be grabbed at a moment's notice in case we had to go. *Go where?* . . . Daily and nightly litany, reciting Uncle Moniek's address in America. "Don't forget it, Marychna! Repeat it. Repeat it again.

Remember, in case we get separated, we will all be writing to Moniek at that address to find each other after the war. OK. What is the address? Please repeat it again."

Two months later, the other shoe fell. During the middle of a late-August night, there was thunderous pounding on our door. A German was loudly screaming obscenities, yelling, "Open the door! Open the door, you dirty Jews, or I'll break it down!" Grandpa Zigmund quickly got out of bed and opened the door. A big brute of a German soldier — or maybe he was SS, I don't know — shoved Grandpa aside and told us to get dressed. He stayed in the room as we scrambled to put on our clothes. "*Schnell, schnell, Juden! Machen Sie schnell!*"—"Fast, fast, Jews! Make it fast!" He continued to yell at us as we were dressing, saying, "You have five minutes to get dressed and pack whatever you can carry and want to take with you! You are being relocated!"

Our five minutes were up. We had managed to get dressed and put on our knapsacks. There was no time left to grab anything else. At gunpoint he ordered us out of our home, and as we walked down the stairs he was right behind us with the carbine cocked and pointed at our backs. Within a few minutes we arrived at our destination, the church directly across the street from our home. Since we didn't have far to go, we were among the first to arrive. We sat down on a wooden pew and watched as every Jewish family in Lubraniec eventually joined us. At last, when they were sure that no one had escaped their search and that we were all assembled in one place, the soldiers fastened shut the church doors and stood guard outside.

We were locked in. They wouldn't let us step outside, not even to use the outhouse. Everyone tried to find a little bit of space for their families. Parents put bundles under their little kids' heads and told them to go to sleep, while they sat upright next to the children. There wasn't enough space for everyone to lie down and the children got priority. Was I one of the kids sleeping, or was I sitting up with the adults? I don't know. It's all blurred together into a hodgepodge of flashbacks, little glimpses of hell that pop up at the most unexpected and sometimes inappropriate times. People huddled on the wooden pews, many of them sitting on the floor, everyone guarding their meager possessions. Some had brought food and drink; others had nothing. Everyone was looking out for their own, yet many of the more fortunate ones shared their food or drink with families who had nothing. We had already realized that the Germans would not give us any food nor even provide us with any water.

Once the long night ended, they opened the church doors and bright sunlight filtered into the sanctuary. We were allowed to step outside into the courtyard, which was surrounded by a solid whitewashed concrete wall, probably four feet high. Many of our Polish neighbors, as well as strangers from the surrounding countryside, had gathered on the sidewalk across the street from the church. The word had quickly spread that all Jews were being held in the church and would not be going back to their homes. Lubraniec was going to be "Jew-free." This brought out the mob for brazen plundering of Jewish homes. We stood enclosed in the church courtyard and watched strangers pass by, loaded down with everything they were able to hoist and carry from our homes. They were dragging furniture, carrying pots, pans, bedding, clothes.

Today I still remember and feel the look of hatred and greed on the faces of those strangers. I can hear their triumphant laughter and vile words: "You Jews are getting what you deserve, you Christ-killers! Good riddance! At last we will be free of you!" Those actions and words can never be erased from my mind. But there was another side to this tragic day. A small percentage of people, many of them our friends and neighbors, stood quietly at the front of the mob, with empty arms. They came out of friendship — to say goodbye and to give us their moral support. Instead of looting our homes, they gave us their sad, tear-stained faces. The woman in whose barn we had buried out treasures was yelling to my mother, over the din, "May God protect you and yours! We will try to salvage some of your possessions, but my friend, the main thing is for you to try and survive through this hell and you and your family come back home to us!" I have never forgotten her words. They became a beacon of hope for me. Yes, there are good people in this world, though it is often the case that we overlook them in the much louder frenzy of hatred. Although I'll never know for sure how much her words had to do with my ultimate survival, this woman was the first of those who, during the ensuing four years of hell, at some of the lowest points in my life, would show me kindness.

We milled around in the courtyard until dusk, when once again the Germans forced us to enter the church, and once again locked us in for the night. On this second night everyone tried to sleep. We were hungry, thirsty, and physically exhausted. In a deep sleep — as though in a dream — I heard German voices yelling at us to get up and form into lines. No, I was not dreaming. It was for real. In the eerie dark of the night, they were giving us orders: "Be quiet! No talking! Move!" Like a group of ghosts, we were marched out past our home, and then past our neighbors' homes and farms, until we were on the outskirts of town. Finally, we reached a spot in the countryside with a single railroad track. After a few minutes we could discern a cattle train. This was our destination.

Now that we were away from a populated area, the Germans became very vocal. Yelling at us, and kicking and beating people who did not move fast enough to please them, the German soldiers forced us at gunpoint to climb up into the cattle cars. Each small car held probably fifty to sixty people. As soon as a car was filled to capacity, the soldiers slid shut its heavy door and locked it from the outside. We managed to create little groups, each family sitting together. A person could sit or stand, but there was no room to lie down or even to consider stretching out one's legs.

Eventually the train started to move. We sat quietly, as mental fatigue, fear, and physical exhaustion took their toll. I sat leaning against the wall and listened to the rhythmic clickety-clack of the wheels as the train chugged along through the dark Polish countryside. I heard sounds and groans from all sides, but it was too dark to see anyone. I must have fallen asleep, and was jarred awake as the train lurched and stopped. Diffused gray daylight cast a little bit of light into our cattle car, throughout which indistinguishable human forms were lumped together. We were all awake, anxiously waiting and hoping for the Germans to open the huge heavy doors and let us out. Nothing happened. No one came. We sat and waited, the fear gnawing at our intestines. *What now?* Nothing.

One brave man stepped gingerly between our cramped bodies and made it to the tiny wired window. It was too high for him to see out, so he lifted a little boy on his shoulders. The kid told us what he saw: farmland, no houses, no roads, just barren countryside, another train track parallel to ours. Nothing else, nothing to identify our location. We sat like that for many hours and then heard another train going past. Shortly after that we were suddenly moving backwards. Our train lurched, stopped, and went forward. We were on the move again. Throughout this whole episode no one from outside ever opened the door or even came near us.

By this time we were in desperate need of bathroom facilities. Some people had brought a cooking pot with them; someone else had a blanket. By crowding on top of each other, we made enough space for two people to hold up the blanket while another person went behind it and relieved himself or herself into the pot. It was very hot inside the car, and to our great dismay the pot quickly filled up with our excrement. The stench was overwhelming. Eventually the train stopped again and this time two German soldiers opened the door and handed us a bucket of water. At gunpoint they permitted one man to climb down and empty the pot of human waste in the fields. They closed the sliding door and again locked it on the outside. Everyone had a few sips of water; we saved the rest for future use. We had no idea how long we would be on the train, no idea whether there would ever be more water.

The pattern established itself. Every few hours our transport train would stop, lurch, move backwards, stop again. Someone figured out that we were being diverted to a side rail so that a more important train with passengers or cargo could travel without disruption. Each of these incidents took hours. I became numb, just sat there and listened to the repetitious clickety-clack of the train. On the second day we got some more water and emptied the slop bucket. After three nights the train stopped and we heard a babble of human voices. Although I could barely discern them, I heard no German, just Polish and Yiddish.

There was a clang as the metal bar was released. Someone was opening the sliding door, the bright daylight blinding us. Before I could form the thought, *What now?* I heard voices saying, in Polish and Yiddish, "Come out, come out. You have arrived in the Łodz ghetto. You will be OK. You are among friends. We are the resettlement committee. Please take all of your possessions and come with us."

Return to Lubraniec

Returning to Lubraniec was not like visiting the other towns. This place held memories of a different nature. But I had to go there and see. After all, Lubraniec was the last place in Poland that I had thought of as home. It held bittersweet memories of my parents and grandparents, scenes of both persecution and kindness. I was fidgety, terrified, and elated on the inside, but sought to be unemotional in my demeanor so that no one, not even my daughters, would have an inkling of my inner turmoil.

When our bus reached the town square, I knew immediately where we were. The local residents disappeared into their stores and homes. They hid behind curtained windows and glared at us. Wloclaw, our tour guide, was very uneasy; he kept saying that we must not linger there. As we walked out of the town square I immediately saw the church across the way. Without hesitation I told everyone that my home was around the corner, on the other side of the street. I had the address with me.

It was very strange to see a wide, well-paved road, rather than the cobbled street of my childhood. Other than that, nothing had changed. Time had stood still. After forty-seven years the church looked just the way I remembered it, and there, across the street, was my home. It turned out that I didn't need to look for the address. As soon as we reached the corner I cried out excitedly, "Look, look! There is the balcony from my parents' bedroom!"

As we got closer, I noticed some changes. The entrance to the alley that led to our apartment was gone, enclosed now by a wall with a built-in gate. There were people inside the building, peering at us with pure hatred in their eyes. No one to talk to, not even to ask one question.

Wloclaw looked very concerned. He wanted to leave, but I had to walk to the end of the street, take a right, find our lumberyard and the adjoining fields. To my surprise, all that land had been developed, filled with what looked like apartments or condominiums. I don't even know for sure whether we saw the railroad track; maybe I just said, "That is where we boarded the cattle train."

We turned around and walked back to our bus, feeling the residents' eyes following our every move as the hatred seemed to pour out of them. At last we left. Wloclaw relaxed, letting us know that he had been afraid of a physical attack by the locals. This was the second and last time that I departed from Lubraniec accompanied by the hatred of the citizens.

Continuing on our journey, we paid a visit to Ciechocinek. Here the people were pleasant, and we had a delightful day walking around the Tenzie and relaxing in a pleasant atmosphere. After fifty years of Soviet Communism, the city looked drab to me. Gone was the splendor that I remembered. I could not find anything of the mineral-water kiosks or the stately spas of my childhood.

Chapter Four

The Łodz Ghetto

1941–1944

Thus began another chapter in my young life. I had no inkling of how much everything would change.

As we disembarked from the train, we were directed into the terminal building and told to stay together in one area and wait for instructions. Three long days and nights of being locked up in the pestilence of a cattle car had transformed most of us into an obedient and submissive group. We had survived without food and with only a few swallows of water. And, after those days and nights without a toilet, any sense of modesty was a thing of the past. We had slept sitting up almost on top of each other. We were hungry, thirsty, exhausted, and apprehensive, having no idea what was to come next.

After what felt like an eternity, a man who was in charge of the "transport and resettlement committee" took center stage and gave us a very long spiel about life in the ghetto and how things operated there. One of the big problems was crowding. The Łodz ghetto, which was less than two square miles in size, was bursting at the seams, filled with a teeming mass of humanity, and the situation was getting steadily worse as hundreds of Jews from surrounding towns and villages were shipped into the ghetto every day.

Near the end, he addressed himself to families with children. The committee could not find housing for new arrivals. Two and three families were already jammed into one-room living quarters. They had nowhere to lodge us. At the orphanage they could provide a temporary home for the children, but the grownups were on their own. As soon as a family found a place to live it could take its children out of the orphanage. Within minutes of this announcement I was separated from my mother and grandparents. All the kids were rounded up, formed into a brigade, and marched to the orphanage.

The kids I was thrown in with were total strangers to me, but they all seemed to know each other and I became the outcast. To make matters worse, they spoke Yiddish, and when I tried to speak to them in Polish they would either ignore me or respond in Yiddish. I didn't know their language — I don't recall having had *any* Jewish friends in Lubraniec — although I did understand some of what they said, since I had managed to learn quite a bit of German during the occupation, and Yiddish and German are very similar. I also had a minimal knowledge of conversational Hebrew, and knew a few words of English from my private studies back home. I tried to answer the kids in German, but quickly learned that speaking German was a big no-no!

Scared and lonely does not even begin to describe my desperation. I had not heard from my mother, and had no idea where she and my grandparents might be. To make things even worse I could not and would not eat the food at the orphanage. For days on end I refused to eat. Every day we were served porridge in the morning and split-pea soup with a couple of pieces of dark bread in the evening, but since early childhood I had never been able to eat porridge or split-pea soup; I had always gagged on them and thrown up. Now that was all there was, so I didn't eat.

My despair, coupled with the lack of food, caught up with me, and I became very ill. Small oozing blisters and boils popped up between my fingers, spreading to my armpits, my elbows, my knees, to every joint of my body. This was accompanied by a high fever. I was told that I had a very contagious infection — commonly referred to as "the itch"— and put in an isolation room. The room was dark and I was the only occupant. No one was allowed to come near me.

I was very ill for probably a week to ten days. One day, after the fever broke, I had a secret visitor. A teenage boy, Chaim, managed to sneak into my room without being caught. He was a few years older than most of us, and I had not been aware that he had been keeping an eye on me before I got sick. When he didn't see me in the dining room for a few days he became concerned, made some inquiries, and found me in the sick bay. He stayed with me for several hours, and we talked about our families, the orphanage, my not eating, and the need for me to get better. Chaim visited me on a daily basis. At last I had a friend, and now I didn't feel so helplessly alone. He convinced me that, if I didn't eat the food we were served, I would not recover and would probably die of starvation. It worked. I promised to eat, and actually started to feel better. Later on, I was allowed to go to the dining hall for all my meals. Chaim sat next to me, supervising, and to my surprise I became very fond of porridge and split-pea soup. Ironically, during the next four years I would have killed to have a bowl of rich soup or porridge. Though I had no way of knowing it, the orphanage was the equivalent of a luxury hotel compared to regular life in the Łodz ghetto.

With Chaim's help I continued to get better. One rainy day I was informed that my mother had arrived at the orphanage and was waiting to take me "home." I saw Chaim a few times after leaving the orphanage, but then lost touch. I have often wondered how he fared in the ghetto, and whether he survived the Holocaust.

I was thrilled to be reunited with my mother. Blabbing non-stop, asking one question after another, I could barely contain myself. "Where are Grandma and Grandpa? Where do we live? What does it look like? Did you know I was sick? Chaim helped me. Do you know Chaim?" Mother hugged me, took my hand, and led me out of the orphanage. My world was good again — I was loved. I was safe with my mother and would soon be with Grandma and Grandpa.

We walked hand-in-hand down some of the ugliest streets I had ever seen. No trees, no grass, no flowers — just concrete sidewalks lined with drab tenement buildings. Each building was connected to the next, and each had a small archway opening onto a courtyard of rock and dirt. They all looked alike, and, when Mother said to me, a little way along, "This is our building," I was amazed that she could distinguish it from the rest of them. Entering through a tunnel-like arch, we emerged into a dreary, muddy, rocky courtyard. Not even a blade of grass dared to grow in such an environment. Gingerly we picked our way over the slippery rocks and pockets of deep mud to the building on our right. At last we were inside a hallway. Instantly I was overwhelmed by its darkness; a terrible reeking stench assailed my senses. Mother pointed to the first door on our left and said, in a matter-of-fact manner, "We live here."

Before I could adjust my eyes from dark to light I heard a din of voices. Mother whispered in my ear, "We all live in this one room. These people were very kind to squeeze together and make room for four more strangers. They let us move in with them until we find a place for just the four of us. We are very lucky. Many families are still homeless." The medium-sized room was occupied by five families. Numerous beds took up every inch of space against the four walls, leaving just enough room between the entry door and our bed for a two-burner, wood-burning stove and a very narrow cupboard with one door. A few makeshift shelves hung above the stove, and in the center of the room stood a small wooden table with four or five chairs. The cupboard held a couple of cooking pots, a few plates and glasses, and no more than half a dozen forks, spoons, and knifes. The shelves were reserved for food, with each family having their own shelf space. At all times at least one member of a family would stay in the room to guard the family food rations. We were all starving, and everyone feared that the other families would steal their food.

The room was bulging at the seams. There were too many people, and not enough beds to accommodate the occupants. A minimum of three to four people slept in each three-quarter bed; these beds, three-quarters the width of a double bed, were standard. My excitement at being back with Mother, Grandma, and Grandpa overshadowed all the stench and horror of the place. The four of us slept in one bed, with Grandma's and Grandpa's heads at one end, and Mother's and mine at the other. Our feet almost touched each others' faces.

The longer we lived in those crowded quarters, the worse it got. Distrust was rampant. People were constantly fighting about the most insignificant things. A crying child could send someone into a rage, exclaiming, "Shut your kid up! If you don't, I will!" Angry voices were always yelling. "Shut up, shut up!" "I want the stove next! Get out of my way!" "Stop pushing!" "Move over!" "Get away from the table! We want to use it now!" "Hey, what are you doing on my shelf?" This went on around the clock. Combined with gut-wrenching hunger, the constant bickering made our lives even more miserable.

In this place of indescribable filth, sewer rats were the only happy inhabitants, traveling freely, spreading diseases throughout the ghetto. Big, bold, and fat, they fed on human excrement. Scurrying around the courtyard, and particularly in and around the outhouse, they were bold enough to attack a child. We had to make a lot of noise to keep them away whenever we had to go.

Despite all the miserable conditions, I quickly adapted to my new life. Mother and Grandpa spent hours hunting for jobs and housing. Grandma got up at dawn to stand in food lines; in fact most of her days were spent in search of food for her family. She usually managed to get a few potatoes or dry beans, which she would combine with whatever else she could scrounge up to make a pot of soup. The soup was our mainstay. A bowl of hot soup, thin though it might be, went a long way; filling our stomachs with liquid somewhat assuaged the ever-present hunger.

Grandpa was the first to get a job. This gave us a little bit of money to buy food on our ration cards, on those rare occasions that it was available. A few weeks later we moved from the crowded first-floor room to an attic in the same building. An old, grotesque-looking woman who lived there by herself invited us to share her space. It was a large, open, roughly finished area with a sloping ceiling and one window. Located above the one-room apartments on the third floor, it could be accessed only by climbing a steep, narrow staircase. But it was light, quiet, and, by ghetto standards, very spacious. No more screaming kids! Mother and Grandpa hung a couple of sheets to separate our two living areas, and we had plenty of room for two three-quarter beds plus a table and chairs. The stove was shared with the old lady. Grandma could cook whenever she wanted to, as long as we had fuel for the stove and food for the pot. Such luxury! The attic felt safe. It became our private refuge.

I was afraid of the old lady, though. Her looks frightened me. Dressed in a black cloak, her distorted, obese body was swollen beyond belief—at the time I thought it was fat—and she had a goiter like a turkey wattle hanging down from below her chin all the way to her chest. I was too young to understand her terrible illness. All I knew was that she scared me to death. She was all alone, probably close to the age of my grandparents, and they were of great comfort to her. As her health continued to decline, Grandma always managed to make a little more soup — if nothing else by adding more water — to take to her bedside.

My grandparents were amazing. Grandpa would make me giggle; he never lost his sense of humor and always made it seem as if life was fine. I was their only grandchild, and together they and I had a mutual-adoration society. They gave me unconditional love, and that love has stayed with me throughout my life. The Nazis could not take that away.

One could not survive in the ghetto without work. Those who worked were compensated with ghetto money, which we needed to purchase whatever bit of food our ration cards allowed. One step removed from complete starvation, we needed work to eke out a bare minimum survival. Grandma Helenka couldn't work, and I was not yet old enough to work in a factory; although Mother and Grandpa Zigmund got jobs, they were insufficient to sustain the four of us. Our situation was very precarious. A temporary solution presented itself when I joined a children's work force, picking weeds in a vegetable field. Each morning our little troop was marched to a field that I believe was outside the ghetto, where we pulled weeds from early morning until late afternoon. Alternating between kneeling and squatting to ease the pain in my knees and back, I moved quietly from one row to the next. There was no camaraderie, no conversation. The guards were quick with their horsewhips if they caught us eating even one vegetable. The slightest imagined misbehavior brought on a lashing. This job lasted until the end of the harvest season. It was my first experience as a slave laborer. I was eleven years old.

By the time I turned twelve — on the 21st of October, 1941 — I had become a tough veteran of the ghetto. Grandpa and Mother were working in factories and trying to find me a job. Unfortunately, before they got very far in their search, I erupted with another case of the itch, this time much worse than before. Huge boils covered most of my body, and the pain was excruciating. I ran a very high fever. There was no medical help. Mother and Grandma took turns sponging my body with cold water and cleaning the pus-filled boils, hoping that I would be able to fight off the infection. All I remember is hearing awful screams, until one day I realized that the screams were coming from me. That was the beginning of my recovery.

As I regained awareness of my surroundings, I noticed that the sheets that separated our room into two areas was gone. The old lady had died during my illness. I had no reaction. Death had become our constant companion, and I was pleased that the attic was ours.

We were very fortunate. Mother found some old family friends. Before the war they had been the owners of a large mercantile factory in Łodz. Now their son held an important position as manager of the ghetto's furniture factory, and he gave my mother a job. In due time he also hired me, despite the fact that I was only twelve and the rules said that you needed to be older. I don't remember what the age restrictions were for working in a factory, but I do remember that under the rules I wouldn't have been old enough for that job, which gave us our much-needed third ration card.

We fell into a daily routine. In the morning, if we were lucky enough to have some fuel for the stove, we would have a cup of ersatz coffee and a slice of bread; if we had no way to cook coffee, we ate just a slice of bread and headed out for work. Grandpa went in one direction, Mother and I in another.

We had a long and often dangerous walk, dangerous because it entailed crossing one of the thoroughfares used by German and Polish traffic for traversing the ghetto. The ghetto sidewalks were separated from the thoroughfares by very high barbed-wire fences, and the crossing points had gates with German guards on both sides of the road. The guards had the power to decide when to stop the traffic and let us cross over to the other side. Often, usually in the hottest days of summer or coldest days of winter, they would hold us back for a long time, until there was a large group waiting to cross. The worse the weather — ice, snow, downpour, or blistering heat — the more the German guards enjoyed watching our suffering. They were sheltered inside their little checkpoint huts, while we were battered by the elements. When they did finally open the gates, the safest way to cross over was in the middle of the group. People on the edges were often beaten just for entertainment. Once we got to the other side we were safe, although of course this procedure would have to occur in reverse on the way home.

When we arrived at the factory, Mother remained on the first floor. She had a desk job, keeping track of production and inventory in the middle of bandsaws and flying sawdust; every person who worked on that floor was covered with a fine film of dust. My job was on the third floor, in the staining and polishing department. The work was physically demanding. All day long a group of us stained bedroom and dining-room furniture. The deep-red mahogany stain, applied by hand, had to be perfectly even, with no perceptible color gradation. Required to meet a daily quota, we stained one piece of furniture after another without a break in the routine. When the stain was completely dry, usually after a couple of days, we then oiled each piece. This process took hours of rubbing, using an oil-soaked chunk of cotton wrapped in cheesecloth, until the surface shone like a mirror and the wood could not absorb another drop of oil. The oil then had to set for a day or two before we applied the final seal and polish; after that each piece was inspected and either passed or rejected by the supervisor. I quickly learned to work at great speed and to produce perfectly finished pieces. "Uneven stain!" "Can you see your face in it?" "It must shine like a mirror!" These were words I did not want to hear, because they were usually accompanied by kicks or other forms of physical abuse. When a piece passed inspection I went back to staining more pieces of furniture, oiling them, and sealing them. This was my life.

Our working conditions were abominable. On the first floor a group of workers made all the wooden parts; on the second floor the parts were assembled; and the finishing process took place on the third floor. The three-story building had no heat during the sub-zero Polish winters, and our hands could barely hold the frozen staining rags. But the third floor was also absolutely the worst place to be during the stifling summer heat; then we could hardly breathe and sweat poured from every pore in our bodies. Winter or summer, one could not see out of the windows, nor open them. They were permanently sealed shut by layers of dirt and grime.

I have a vague memory of a factory whistle announcing lunchtime. This half hour was our only break during the work day. Every laborer grabbed his or her lunch bowl and proceeded to the courtyard. There we formed a line that led to an open window, where a woman stood with a huge cauldron of soup. She poured one ladle of soup into each outstretched bowl. Depending on the availability of food supplies in the ghetto we either had soup with some substance to it, like beans and barley, or a bowl of mostly liquid with a few pieces of vegetables. Potatoes were our most prized staple, and to get a bowl of soup with some potatoes in it was the goal of every worker. Depending on the woman's mood and whether she liked you, she would either give you mostly liquid from the top, or dip way down into the cauldron and fill your bowl with something more substantial. Either way, this one bowl of soup per day was our lifeline to survival.

Despite all the misery and hard work, I still managed to have friends, though we didn't play games like normal kids. Instead we stood in lines with our ration cards, hoping to maybe get lucky and be one of the fortunate ones who got some meat before the butcher ran out, since he rarely had enough for everyone. The quota was just a quarter kilogram of horse meat or sometimes pork per person per month, but one could wait in lines for hours and go home empty-handed. We got a small loaf of bread per week, and there were rations of potatoes, flour, sugar, ersatz coffee, and at times barley, beans, turnips, or kohlrabi. Never did we have all of these foods at the same time. Sometimes flour, at other times barley or potatoes, but in any case never enough to satisfy our hunger. Occasionally we received a quarter kilogram of fat, which would have to last for weeks. Basically that was all the food we ate in the ghetto. There were no vegetables other than those mentioned above, with the exception of an occasional head of cabbage or some beets. From the time when I first entered the Łodz ghetto in September 1941, until April 15, 1945, I never saw or ate fresh fruit, milk, an egg, or any kind of snack.

The situation in the ghetto was getting worse, as day after day new transports arrived — not only from various Polish towns but also from Germany and other countries — increasing the population density.

Crammed into a small area that had been the Łodz slums before the war, surrounded by tall barbed-wire fencing constantly patrolled by German police, we were essentially in a top-security prison, from which only a few managed to escape. At one time there were almost a quarter of a million of us, all suffering from malnutrition and disease. The death toll was staggering. My nightmares are full of dead bodies being carted off by subhuman-looking men, usually two of them, pulling a wagon full of the deceased. The bodies would be piled high, and sometimes one would fall off as the men pulled the wagon forward. My brain can't erase the pictures of dead eyes staring open, rigid arms and legs, human corpses piled on top of each other. Death didn't discern between the young and old. They all had the same look, with sunken eyes, protruding bones, and skeletal bodies.

Suddenly there was a change. In the summer of 1942, instead of more people being transported into the ghetto, there began to be transports out of the ghetto. The transports started by taking children from the orphanage, proceeded with the liquidation of the hospital, and then moved on to the elderly. No one felt safe. Rumors were flying. At the beginning we had no idea where those who were deported were being taken, and as we learned more we still did not want to believe that even the Germans were capable of such mass murder. Shipments of clothing were coming into the ghetto, which workers had to sort for distribution. A mother recognized her little girl's dress; soon other workers were identifying familiar clothing. "Why are they sending back our children's clothing?" "Oh this was my mother's coat, my grandma's dress. . . ." We knew!

Chaim Rumkowski, the chairman of the Łodz ghetto government, made speeches. "The Germans are demanding quotas from us. We have to select who will be on the next transport, but I am doing this to save you, the workers. . . . As long as we work and produce, the Germans will not liquidate the whole Łodz ghetto. All the workers are safe."

Posen 27.10.1941

Sehr Lieber Mauritz u. Hantka!

Ich habe schon längst an Euch nicht geschrieben. Seit den 25.6. d. J. befinde mich in Posen. Ich sei hier als Sanitäter in ein Arbeits-Lager beschäftigt. mir ist nicht schlecht. Ich bin Gesund u. Arbeit tüchtig. Auto, Miriam u. die l. Eltern befinden sich seit d. 27.9. in Litzmanstadt (Łódz) Ich habe einige Briefe von die schon erhalten. Gott sei Dank dass alle Gesund sind. Ich verhoffe dass Ihr gleich an sie schreiben wird auch mit ein wenig Geld stixe beihilfig sein. Sonst was macht Ihr meine Teuere guts

Absender:
Fr. Kominkowski
Posen, Deutsches Reich
Fort Radziwill

Ich verhoffe von Euch
Antwort zu erhalten.
Ich grüße u. küsse
Euch sehr herzlich
Euer Zutu.
Herzliche grüsse für
der gesamter Familie

Mr. M. Jacobs-Jacobi
7422 N.E. Glisan St.
Portland, Oregon
U.S.A.

Z. Kominkowski

Posen, German Reich

Fort Radziwill

Posen, October 27, 1941

Very Dear Mauritz and Hanita,

I haven't written to you for quite some time. Since June 25 of this year, I find myself in Posen. I am here as a medical orderly in a work camp. I am not doing too badly. I am in good health and work with enthusiasm.

Ruta, Miriam, and the two parents find themselves in Litzman-stadt (Łodz) since September 27. I have received some letters from them. Thank god they are all healthy. I hope that you will write to them immediately; also a little money would be helpful.

Other than that, how are you, my good friends? I hope to receive an answer from you. I greet and kiss you wholeheartedly.

Your Zalmen

Heartfelt greetings to the whole family.

A postcard from my father to Uncle Moniek and Aunt Hanita. He would have composed his message to survive censorship by the Germans.

Despite Rumkowski's assurances, the deportations continued to escalate. Our own Jewish ghetto police were performing random searches, block by block, for children and the elderly. The process was simple: policemen surrounded an entire block at a time, went into the complex of buildings, and with a loudspeaker ordered every inhabitant to report to the courtyard. After the selection, the police followed up with a room-by-room search, looking for those who might be in hiding.

On September 12, 1942, the police cordoned off our block. Mother, Grandma, Grandpa, and I were all in the attic when we heard a commotion in the courtyard below our window. Someone was yelling, "There's a selection going on, right now on our block! They are two buildings from us! Hide the children!" There must have been a coordinated plan of action among everyone who lived in our apartment compound, because within a couple of minutes men were carrying a ladder up the stairs to the landing outside our attic home. As soon as they had it set up, a man climbed up the ladder and opened an almost invisible trap door in the ceiling of the landing, leading to a crawl space directly above our room. I became aware that a few children I didn't know had followed the men up the stairs. These kids and I were ordered to climb up the ladder into the rafters, crawl in as far as we could, and lay down flat on our bellies. We were not to make a sound. If we weren't discovered by the police someone would come back with the ladder and get us. "Lay as flat as possible and spread out. Do not be close to each other. If you hear footsteps or someone opening the trap door don't move or make a single sound. It might be the police. If it's one of us we'll let you know. Now scoot fast." With that, the trap door shut behind us and we were in total darkness.

The crawl space had maybe two feet of head room, and we couldn't have stood or sat up even if we had wanted to. I crawled on my belly, feeling invisible in the black space. The other kids must have done the same. We maintained total silence. I could feel my heart pounding as spiders and vermin crawled all over me. Cold sweat covered my face. I could see nothing in the blackness, though I could taste the dust and smell the rat droppings. I never made a sound or moved my body; all my attention was focused on listening for sounds below us. All was quiet. We waited and waited for what seemed like eternity when suddenly I heard something. It sounded like the ladder was being set up to the trap door. *They're searching the building and they've discovered the trap door. Oh, my, they are going to find us. Hold your breath, hold your breath, don't move. If they call out, don't answer.* This litany was running through my head as I lay there waiting for the unknown. If I was invisible, maybe somehow I would not get caught. Time had no meaning; it stood still, waiting with me to discover my fate.

After what seemed like a lifetime, I heard footsteps on the ladder and someone opening the trap door. Before I had a chance to form a thought, a familiar male voice was calling to us, "OK kids, come out. You're safe. They're gone. Come to the ladder. It's safe." Slithering on my belly towards the light, I reached the ladder, scampered down, and walked into our room, expecting to be back with my family. Instead of my mother or grandparents I saw a very old woman, cowering in a corner of the room. I recognized her as someone who lived with her daughter one floor below us. She had been bedridden for as long as we had lived in the attic, but now had managed somehow to crawl up the steep flight of stairs to our room. She looked at me and said, childishly, "I am hiding." I told her to go back to her own place and ran downstairs. The courtyard was full of people, and it took me a couple of minutes to spot my mother, standing forlornly by herself amidst our neighbors.

Grandma had been chosen for the selection, and Grandpa had immediately followed her to the truck. On that particular day my grandparents were the only casualties in our complex. Had they remained in the attic they would have survived for a little bit longer. Grandma, though, had refused to stay in the attic, afraid that if the building was searched and she was found, it would lead to a closer inspection of the area that in all probability would endanger the hidden children. Staunch-ly she went to the selection, knowing that she would most likely be put on the transport. Short and stout, and looking old and worn, she was the perfect candidate for deportation from the ghetto. Grandpa, on the other hand — tall, dapper, and fit — was not selected, but Mother told me that he voluntarily, and without hesitation, accompanied his wife to the truck and to what he knew was certain death for both of them.

Mother and I had one slight hope: to find where they were being detained and then to quickly reach our friend the director of the furniture factory and beg for his intervention. We found the detention area, but by the time we got there my grandparents had already been transferred into bigger trucks and transported out of the ghetto. Rumors abounded as to their destination. We knew that Jews were being murdered by the thou-sands, but not how and where. It would not be until many years later that I would learn their fate.

With the loss of my grandparents, I went through an immediate trans-formation. I was still only twelve years old, and even though I had been working for months under terrible conditions at the furniture factory, Grandma and Grandpa took care of me when I returned to our attic. Now the sheltered little girl was gone. Within hours I lost the last ves-tige of childhood, assuming the role of Mother's protector. She really fell apart, and now I had to take care of her. Grieving together, we went back to work and returned to our attic, but our home was devoid of life.

In the middle of the following winter, we found a tiny room in an-other enclave, directly across the street from our factory. I organized the move, and friends helped me. We dragged the three-quarter bed down the three flights of stairs, turned it upside down to create a sled, piled our few belongings onto the cross-boards, tied it all up with rope, and pulled the whole kit and caboodle along the snowy, ice-covered streets across the ghetto and past the crossing points to our new home.

We were alone, but determined to survive. Our relationship, though, had changed dramatically. We functioned no longer as mother and little girl, but much more as partners in survival. She was still my mother and I her daughter, of course, but I now took the leadership role and with it responsibility for procuring our rations. Mother's physical condition had deteriorated, and it was up to me to stand in the ration lines and fight with the best and worst of the others for our share of food.

The move was very good for us. The tiny, cramped space — at the most the room was no more than eight feet wide by ten feet long — barely held our bed, a small chest of drawers, and a little round table with three chairs. A two-burner wood stove occupied a corner spot between the foot of our bed and the wall at the end of the room, and a few shelves above the stove held our cooking utensils and groceries. The latter were quite meager: a little container of flour, another with maybe half a cup of sugar, a small loaf of bread that had to last for a week, salt, some ersatz coffee, and once in a while a quarter cup of oil. Those were our staples, supplemented by the other rationed goods described earlier.

Our new life had a few advantages. The room was so small that in the winter, as soon as we would start the stove to cook something, the space would warm up to above freezing temperature and be almost bearable. Since our factory was located directly across the street, there were no more dangerous crossing points. It took only two minutes to get to work, which gave us another hour of sleep in the morning and more time at home after work.

We made new friends, and my mother met and befriended an elderly German Jewish professor who had arrived on a transport from Germany. He became a frequent visitor. The professor had no family or friends, did not speak Polish, and was very isolated, but he reminded me of Grandpa. He and Mother conversed in German, and she treated him with great deference. In the meantime I was busy reading books from the ghetto library, which was located fairly close to our home. There weren't very many kids' books, so I discovered some of the great Russian writers. I became enthralled with communism, and couldn't get enough of this utopian philosophy. I was also very busy knitting skirts and sweaters. As soon as I outgrew one piece of clothing I would unravel the yarn and knit something else that would fit. It was the ghetto form of recycling!

Despite the starvation, disease, and deaths, despite fearing the constant transports out of the ghetto, we somehow managed to have some culture. There was the Yiddish theater, usually a spoof on ghetto life, and full of self-deprecating humor. We had poets and song writers, and every few weeks there was another hit tune being sung by all of us. *Ignore the death wagons, disease, and starvation. Live, live, live, until they either put you on a transport or cart away your stinking carcass.*

The professor didn't come around anymore. One day he visited us and the next day he had vanished into the unknown. The rats were busy scurrying around in the courtyard, and I sat by the window, knitting and watching them. Spring came. I met a pretty girl with rosy red cheeks, reclining on a folding chair in the courtyard. My age, she lived upstairs. She didn't work and needed a lot of rest. One day, as we sat visiting, she had a terrible coughing bout, and I saw bright red foam running out of her mouth. "Oh, that," she said. "I have tuberculosis." Soon she no longer came out anymore. After work I would go upstairs and spend some time with her. She got worse and worse, becoming too ill even to raise her head. One day, when I made my usual trip up the stairs, her mother opened the door but did not let me in. Instead, devoid of any expression, she said, "My daughter died last night. The body squad came today and took her away." With that she turned away from me and shut the door. The tuberculosis had invaded my friend's entire body, attacking all her bones and organs. The red cheeks had been a sign, not of good health, but of tubercular disease. I was sad, but took the news without much emotion. We had been friends, and now she was no more. I had become totally accustomed to living with loss.

On a warm and sunny day—I don't know what month or year—I overheard some people talking about a transport of men who were being held in the deportation depot. They were from a labor camp in Poznań, now on the way to some other place, with a temporary stop in the Łodz ghetto. This was most unusual, and why they were in the ghetto I will never know. As soon as I heard the words "from a labor camp in Poznań," I started running to the deportation center. With my heart pounding and my pulse racing, my whole being was focused on the possibility that my father might be there. I was sure that these men were from the same labor camp, Camp Radziwill! As soon as I reached the enclosure I started yelling his name. I was on the outside, separated from the men within by a very tall wire fence. No one was near the fence. I saw little groups of men—or should I say walking skeletons—inside the enclosure and too far away from me to be recognizable. The only thing that I could do was to keep yelling my father's name, hoping that someone would respond. Maybe, just maybe, my daddy was one of them.

At last I saw a man detach himself from the group and start walking toward me. It wasn't really a walk, more of a shuffle; he seemed to have an injured leg that he had to drag along the ground. Slowly he reached the area across from me, on the other side of the fence. I was in shock. This man looked like he was a hundred years old. Covered with filth and grime, he had fingers that looked like claws, and sunken cheeks with black holes that once had held his teeth. In a dry and raspy voice he asked, "Who are you? Why do you ask for Zalmen Kominkowski?"

I told the man that Zalmen Kominkowski was my father. Suddenly there was a light in his blank and staring eyes. He said, "Your father is dead. I knew him in the camp. He was an angel! We had a typhus epidemic in the camp. Your father nursed all the sick and dying. He never rested. He worked day and night trying to bring comfort to them. Three days after the epidemic ended your father got sick. He died within a couple of days. What you see here are the men who survived the epidemic.

That's all that is left out of hundreds of us. Be grateful that your father died. Look at us. We are being sent to the gas chambers because we are too weak and sick to do any more work. You had a beautiful father; be grateful that he doesn't have to face this final indignity. We are being shipped out of here in a few hours, to a place called Auschwitz."

With this said, the skeleton shuffled away. I went home and never told my mother about this experience. I wanted her to have hope that Daddy was still alive. Still, I have always had the feeling that she knew, and that she also kept the bad news to herself. Each of us wanted the other to have hope.

We continued to exist. Mother had heart attacks; I was diagnosed with a case of tuberculosis. Miraculously, without rest or medication, my cough waned and I was OK. I was determined to live and take care of my mother. I knew that she would die without me, and so I lived and functioned.

Skinny, small, and terribly undernourished, I fought anyone who tried to take advantage of my size and push ahead of me in the food lines. I walked on the dangerous sidewalk along the barbed-wire fence that closed off the ghetto from one of the main arteries for German and Polish traffic. Instead of a street crossing like the one in our previous location, we now had the famous Łodz ghetto bridge. This bridge, probably two stories high and extremely slippery and icy in the winter, was a connection to a different part of the ghetto, and I needed to cross it in order to get to the vegetable depot. I had to climb the bridge, descend on the opposite side, and once again traverse along the barbed-wire fence in order to get our sack of potatoes or whatever vegetables — most often turnips or kohlrabi — were available. These usually came packed in bags weighing about twenty or thirty pounds, and I would throw the heavy sack over my shoulder and retrace my walk home. This was a physically demanding task. Going up and down the slippery, ice-covered stairs was fairly easy for me, but even though I was very agile the return trip was fraught with danger. Carrying the sack of produce slung over my shoulder, I could easily slip and lose my precious cargo. It was not uncommon for someone to trip you just so they could grab your food, and there was the additional danger that you might be shot from the thoroughfare. That was done strictly for sport: kill a Jew. We were always fair game.

Memories of the Łodz ghetto have stayed with me, as vivid today as they were more than sixty years ago. The death carts were everywhere, filled beyond capacity, the stiffened corpses falling off the carts and the men stopping to throw them back on. Eventually the carts would disappear around the corner, but within a few hours more dead bodies lay on the sidewalks, waiting for the wagons. It was an ongoing daily process. Cart away one batch, turn around, and come back for more. This ritual was an integral part of the ghetto landscape, a vision I learned to ignore.

We were alive and that was all that mattered. Another day at the factory, maybe go to the Yiddish theater or read a book—somehow we were still full of hope. We had survived another day; it didn't matter that we were skin and bones. In the fall we celebrated my thirteenth birthday. Mother was a miracle worker, making cookies for the special occasion out of grated potato skins and one teaspoon of chocolate that she had somehow managed to buy on the black market. She made six cookies and invited our neighbors to the party.

That year passed quickly for us. Oh yes, there were daily roundups, and because they had already emptied the ghetto of the sick, the old, and most of the children, no one was safe. The ghetto government would be given a quota for deportation, which they had to fill. Without notice a factory would have a roundup and most of the workers in that factory would be put on a transport, never to be heard from again. Poof! They disappeared into thin air, though a few managed to escape and hide.

By the summer of 1944, our factory was one of only a few that were still functioning. The ghetto streets were devoid of life. We hugged the buildings, trying to be invisible whenever we had to venture out to the bakery for our weekly loaf of bread. I don't recall much about any other food by this time, even though I know that we must have had some.

We heard the stories of Auschwitz, and we knew that the Warsaw ghetto had been liquidated. Chairman Rumkowski kept reassuring us that as long as we worked we were safe. Speaking about the liquidation of the Warsaw ghetto, he said that they did not have factories, and we did. He was convinced that working in the factories would save us; after all, we were producing goods for the Fatherland. We wanted to believe. We had to delude ourselves. The ghetto was becoming a ghost town. At one point there had been more than two hundred thousand of us, and now we were down to a few thousand. Rumors had it that the Russian army was getting closer; we might be liberated within a few weeks. *Hang on, hang on. We must live. . . .* Forget that we were human skeletons, scarecrows dancing the danse macabre, forcing ourselves to keep alive until liberation. We were barely holding on to life, waiting, but not sure for what. Liberation — or maybe a trip to an extermination camp.

Our building was almost empty. I sat by the window staring out at the scurrying rats in the deserted courtyard. No more friends or neighbors; if they were still alive they would also be hiding in their rooms. In the middle of one late-August night in 1944 we were awakened by a gentle knocking on our door. Mother's friend, the director of the furniture factory, was softly calling her name. As soon as he was in our room, he told Mother that under no circumstances were we to go to work. He had gotten word that our factory was going to be liquidated as soon as all the workers were inside the building. He told us to get dressed and to grab whatever food we had left, as well as our blanket and pillows, and to go under the cover of darkness to the third tenement building away from ours. Under one of the rooms a couple of men had dug a cellar in which to hide their families, and we could join them. The factory director's parting words were, "My son, sister, and mother are already there, as well as a couple of other families. I'll be in touch." With that last sentence, he left.

Mother made me put on three dresses, one on top of the other. I never questioned, just did as she told me. She, also, put on multiple layers of clothing. We grabbed our pillows, our goose-feather blanket, and our almost nonexistent food, and left our very last home. This process took maybe half an hour. It was still dark outside as we carefully slunk along the building walls, trying to blend into them, hoping not to be spotted by the ghetto patrol. Within a few minutes we arrived safely at our destination. A man let us in and said, "We've been expecting you." He moved a chair and the floor rug underneath it, exposing a trap door to the cellar. He opened it and told us to go down. Within seconds the trap door closed above us, and we heard the sounds of the rug being thrown back into place, as well as the scraping sounds the chair made as it was being dragged back across the floor to its original position.

The space was lit by one candle. I could barely see all the people gathered in this small, dank, earthy space, basically just a big hole dug out under a room. Mother and I found a vacant spot of earth, which we immediately occupied. This now became our home. Daily life consisted of sometimes having a bite of food and occasionally something to drink. Most of the time I lay curled up into a little ball and slept. Sleep became my friend, making hunger and thirst more manageable; bathroom urges were few due to the lack of food and water, and dreams were big, and bold, and beautiful. I dreamt of freedom, of being reunited with my father, but most often my subconscious turned to food, especially huge platters of scrambled eggs.

The days passed, one after another. We waited for the Russians. A young man would come in the middle of the night, usually around two AM, to bring us news and to let someone go up to empty our toilet bucket. Once in a while he would bring a few pieces of bread. One night, though, he didn't come at two. We were all awake, and the later it got the more fearful we became, but no one could venture out of the cellar without some assistance from the outside. At last, at about four in the morning, as we were almost beyond hope, we heard noises above us. We were afraid to breathe, sure that it was the ghetto police searching the premises. Someone was pulling the chair across the floor. There were no voices. *Are they trying to trap us by being quiet?* As these thoughts were racing through my mind, I and everyone in the cellar heard the opening of the trap door. We had already extinguished the candle light and sat in total darkness. *Is this the end?*

Before I could form the whole thought, I heard the familiar voice of our young man. Apologizing for being late, he told us of the latest development in the ghetto. There were no more civilians left except for some groups in hiding. The Germans had offered chairman Rumkowski a passenger train for himself, the other titular heads of the ghetto, the ghetto police, and all of their families. They promised relocation and factory work in Germany as a thank-you to all those people who had been so devoted to producing goods for German consumption. Rumkowski, of course, would continue to be the leader after the move. He and the others had agreed to take the German offer, since there was no sign of an approaching Russian army.

Our young man had come to inform us that we could join them as part of the family group. Should we opt not to go, we would be on our own. If we decided to join the group, we had to be at the train depot by six AM. He made sure that we understood that this would be the last train out of the Łodz ghetto. Our group consisted of mostly women and children, and we knew that our survival odds were almost nil if we stayed behind without any outside help. Besides, Rumkowski was going and he was pretty sharp. We chose to join him.

Mother had been very smart to make me wear the three dresses. We were told to leave all our possessions in the cellar. The young man instructed us: "Carry nothing. Walk single file and try to blend in with the buildings. If you are spotted by the ghetto police or the SS you will be immediately shot. The ghetto is under marshal law and they are killing

94

everyone." We climbed up the ladder, without looking back. Remembering the young man's words, we proceeded carefully to the train station.

As soon as we entered the terminal, we knew that we had chosen the wrong option. We were immediately surrounded by the SS with their vicious German shepherd police dogs. Their guns pointing directly at us, they were yelling, "*Schnell! Schnell! Raus, Juden!*" They pushed us out onto the train platform, where I immediately saw awaiting us, not a passenger train, but a very long cattle train. The dogs were barking. The SS were hitting people with their rifles and screaming obscenities.

For the second time in my life I climbed into a cattle car. Remembering our first cattle-car experience, I managed to pull my mother with me as I fought our way to a side wall. I knew that with no one behind us and a wall to lean against for back support, and surrounded by people on only three sides, we had slightly better odds of survival. Backs against the wall, legs stretched out in front, we were trying to establish our territory. Good idea, but it didn't work. More and more people were being shoved into the crowded space. Eventually we sat with our knees bent and almost pulled up to our chests. By the time the Germans locked us in, there were probably a hundred people in our cattle car. This time there wasn't even a pot to use as a toilet. Even if we'd had one, there was not a spare inch of space for such niceties. As the train pulled away from the station, I still had hope that, even though we were in a cattle train, it didn't mean that we were not going to a work camp.

Return to Łodz

On August 29, 1944, my mother and I had been on the very last transport that carried people out of the Łodz ghetto and brought them to Auschwitz. Decades later I had learned that when my beloved Grandma Helenka and Grandpa Zigmund were taken away they had been put on one of the transports to the Chelmno extermination camp. When they got there, they were murdered by the infamous lethal gas vans, vehicles rigged so that their exhaust could be piped directly into the interior, killing all those inside as they arrived. The bodies were then dumped into mass graves in the nearby woods.

Now our little group was going to Łodz, which for me would be returning to the site of my family's dissolution. My emotions were tumultuous and powerful. Coming here meant coming back to a place of overwhelming loss, but also I could hardly wait to show my girls where I had lived and worked. I was excited to show them my bridge, the one that I had had to cross so many times, going back and forth on the treacherous journey to and from the food lines.

Łodz was ugly, and extremely unwelcoming. It was a dirty and dreary city, mostly in shades of gray — just like my memories of the ghetto.

To my great disappointment, I could not find a single familiar landmark in Łodz. The bridge had been torn down; just this fact alone left me disoriented. Even though I had the addresses, all of the streets had been named in German by the occupying forces and then were renamed back to

Polish after the liberation. We couldn't find either one of the buildings I had lived in, nor could we find the factory.

All my expectations were shattered. I had a great need to show my girls where and how I had lived for three years of my childhood. Not only could we not find our homes or any evidence of the furniture factory, there was nothing even left anywhere in Łodz to indicate that once upon a time more than two hundred thousand captive Jews had lived there, dying from disease and starvation.

We spent a few hours at the Jewish cemetery. Wloclaw was quite concerned and visibly uncomfortable the whole time. That particular area of Łodz was not at all safe, and we were all glad to board our bus and go back to the hotel.

I could hardly wait to depart from Łodz.

Chapter Five

AUSCHWITZ

1944

Stifling hot air, filled with the smell of vomit, human excrement, and eventually dead bodies, permeated the interior of our cattle car. The car had no windows, and only bits of daylight came through the cracks; we sat there for days in almost total darkness. At least a hundred people were crammed into the same amount of space that had held fifty or sixty of us when we were transported from Lubraniec to the Łodz ghetto in 1941. After three years of life in the ghetto we were a sad-looking bunch of skeletal human beings. Now, without food or water, and sitting in our own excrement, many among us were physically ill and dying. We departed the Łodz ghetto on the morning of August 29th, and arrived at our destination early in the morning of September 2nd. Against all odds, some of us survived this ordeal.

The rhythmic noise of the wheels was periodically interrupted by a sudden stop. We'd sit for hours without moving, and then suddenly the train would lurch and off we went again. The last time it stopped was different from the others, and we realized that we had arrived at our destination. We heard loud German voices yelling orders, and then the heavy door of our cattle car was unlocked and slid open. Before we could adjust our eyes to the bright daylight from the darkness we had become accustomed to, the SS were yelling, *"Raus Juden! Raus! Schnell! Machen Sie schnell!!"* Crawling over a couple of dead bodies, Mother and I made our way to the open door. The platform was probably three feet beneath us. Before jumping down, I saw German soldiers with police dogs standing maybe six to ten feet apart along the whole length of the train. Their rifles were cocked and pointing at us. A slight distance behind the soldiers was a nice-looking brick building, surrounded by yellow flower beds. It all looked so innocent. My first thought was, *This looks like a fairly nice work camp. It will be OK. Surely nothing can be worse than what we have just experienced. We can still stand up. We made it.*

The Germans were barking orders: "Women and children go left! Men go to the right! March! Move, move! Form a line! Keep quiet! No talking!" Suffering from shock and exhaustion, we silently obeyed them. Evidently our car had been a long way from the front of the train. We stood in an unbelievably long line of women and children, and there were many more behind us. Although we had been ordered to be quiet, no talking, an almost inaudible whisper like a rustle of dry leaves ran up and down the line: "Auschwitz. We are in Auschwitz." We had heard rumors about it. Occasionally a few people had managed to slip in and out of the ghetto, and some of them had brought back news about gas chambers and crematorium ovens.

As our line inched slowly forward, I saw an SS officer standing slightly in front of two other SS who flanked him on either side. He was obviously in charge. One at a time the women walked toward him. With the flick of his finger he sealed their fate. I saw that all of the elderly, frail, and children were being sent to his right. The younger and somewhat healthier-looking females were ordered to his left. Knowing from ghetto selections that the healthier-looking females were probably being chosen for slave labor and therefore had a better chance of survival, I made it my goal to pass to his left (our right). My odds weren't very good. I was fourteen years old, but I looked like a little girl. Three years of abuse and starvation had taken a tremendous toll on my development: I had not yet reached puberty, and in fact had the body of a child of ten or eleven. My thick, long, chestnut-colored hair was plaited into two braids. Quickly I undid them, shook my hair out, and used the ribbon from the braids to tie the bottom of my hair, pulling it under and up to create a pageboy effect, hoping that it would make me look older. I was still wearing the three dresses, which gave me a heavier and healthier appearance.

Mother made me walk in front of her. If I was sent to the officer's right, she would follow me; they did not stop anyone from trying to go in that direction. Watching the selection as we got closer to the front, I thought that my mother would probably be sent to the slave-labor side. Despite her ill health and all the other hardships she had endured, she was still a strikingly beautiful thirty-nine-year-old woman, and a prime prospect for at least a few months of forced labor. I was afraid that without me she would give up and not survive. I had to—I just had to pass the selection and stay with her. Together we had a chance to make it. Before I knew it, it was my turn to step up in front of the SS. Head held high, I met his gaze and even managed a little smile. His forefinger pointed to his left, and I marched to what I thought was the good side. Mother followed me. We had passed our first inspection into Auschwitz!

Surrounded by guards, we stood waiting. When the selection was complete they ordered us to form lines five deep, at arms' length from each others' sides and from front to back. "No talking! Stand at attention!" We were counted and re-counted, then marched through an iron gate into an area surrounded by double barbed-wire fences. We marched and marched and marched until we came to a stop in front of a building. At that point the woman who had been leading us announced that we had arrived at the showers. "Take off all your clothes! You're filthy from the long ride. Your clothes will be disinfected and waiting for you after you've showered." We obeyed. Actually we had no choice: you could get beaten or killed right now, or do as they say and maybe be lucky and live. We had heard many stories about Auschwitz, including the famous "showers" that weren't showers at all but gas chambers. Walking single-file in almost total darkness between what felt like two walls, my naked body pressing against the one in front of me while Mother pressed mine from behind, I remember shuffling around what felt like curves and turns. It also seemed as if we were going downhill. Once again, fear permeated us. Whispered questions: "Are we really going to have a shower, or is this the gas chamber?" There were no answers, of course, only questions.

Was it a lifetime, or only an hour or two, before I reached an opening into a long, narrow room? Both long walls were mirrored, and facing each wall of mirrors was a row of evenly spaced chairs maybe two to three feet apart. Each chair was occupied by a woman whose hair was being shaved off, down to the bare skull, by a "barber." The scene was surreal. The barbers were young, healthy-looking inmates with their own hair intact and flowing down their backs. It took no more than a minute to rid a new arrival of all her hair, and the turnover was quick and efficient. My turn came to sit in one of those chairs; Mother was sent to another open seat and we got separated. After shaving my head, the barber dipped a short handheld mop into a bucket full of slimy green liquid and applied it to my head, armpits, and crotch. She informed me that it was a "disinfectant," to "prevent disease." I've never forgotten the burning sensation as the foul liquid ran down my face and burned my eyes. Then I was told to go to the end of the room and stand with the other women whose heads had been shaved. Every woman in our group experienced the same degradation. We had been stripped of all personal identity.

Separated from my mother, I was in the midst of a tightly packed group that was getting bigger and bigger. Ultimately there were hundreds of women, and all I could hope for was that Mother was among them. We were standing facing the back wall, my view limited to the bare back of the woman in front of me. There was an entrance in that wall to another area, and when it was opened we were ordered to move forward. Guards behind us beat the backs of the women closest to them, creating a momentum of pushing and shoving forward to avoid the beating.

When we were all inside, the door clanged shut behind us. We were packed like a tin of sardines, our bodies touching. I looked up and saw sprinkler heads in the ceiling. *Are those real water sprinklers or the fake showers that dispense gas?* Every one of us was terrified, waiting for the end. Crying and screaming, some of the women praying, we awaited our fate. I felt so alone and lost without my mother next to me. I didn't want to die without saying goodbye to her. Barely had these thoughts formed when I heard a snakelike hiss. The wailing increased to a crescendo with screams rising to a shrieking din: "Oh my god! It's the gas! They're killing us!" A drop fell on my head as the shower heads opened up and sprayed us with water. I tipped back my head, letting the blessed, life-saving liquid pour over my face and into my parched mouth. Now there were screams of joy!

A couple of minutes later the water was turned off. Another door opened, this time leading to an outside courtyard. We were ordered out and stepped into daylight. In the center of the courtyard, surrounded by a chicken-wire fence probably three feet high, was a pile of clothing. We were told to form a line, single file. Women inmates stood on top of the pile, and as we walked past them, they threw each one of us a single item of clothing. A bit farther along, another woman was throwing shoes at us. I was the recipient of a little girl's pin-striped navy-blue dress, with a white Peter Pan collar and matching cuffs. Even though I was short and undernourished, the dress barely covered my naked body. The shoes were a different story; huge, with clunky heels, they wouldn't stay on my feet. Together the dress and shoes became my Auschwitz uniform.

I knew from the style and size of the items that their previous owners must have gone directly to the gas chambers. They never had a chance to survive. Those shoes and the dress told their own stories. A young girl, an old woman — their lives had no value to the Nazis. A child at the beginning of her young life and an old woman in the twilight of her years are two of the approximately one million people murdered in Auschwitz. Who were they? We'll never know. To the Nazis the only value they had was in the gold tooth fillings extracted from their dead bodies. How much money did that bring into German coffers? Today, looking back, I can afford these questions. In Auschwitz in 1944 at the age of fourteen I did not have the knowledge or probably the maturity to ponder them, and even if I had understood more, would not have had the luxury. I had to live, and to do that I had to focus every ounce of energy on my own survival. All I knew was that neither the dress nor the shoes fit me, and that I needed to find my mother.

A throng of women with shaved heads and dressed in bizarre-looking clothes was milling around the courtyard. I told myself over and over again that Mother must be among them, and that I just had to find her. Without hair or clothing it was difficult to recognize our loved ones, but there was something familiar in the carriage and back of a woman dressed in a man's white, one-piece long johns. Pushing my way through the crowd, I tried to reach her. As I got closer, she turned around and our eyes met. It was my mother! I had found her! Overwhelmed with relief and joy we hugged and kissed, not wanting to let go for what seemed like forever. At last we backed off to arms' length and studied each others' appearance. Within a few seconds, in the midst of that nightmare, we burst into hysterical laughter. Both of us looked ludicrous. Our sense of humor served us well: we were together and we could still laugh, and for the moment that was enough.

When every woman in our group was "dressed," we had to once again stand in rows of five and be counted. Then we went on yet another long march to our living quarters, in *Lager* A. I put one weary foot in front of the other, keeping in perfect step with the rest of our column. We had now gone for most of another day without food or water (except what we had swallowed in the shower). We marched past row upon row of identical, ugly, one-story wooden buildings, until finally we stopped in front of one and were told that this one was our "home." Those buildings were long and narrow, without windows and with only one door at the front for entry and exit. Inside, separating the building into two halves, was a narrow aisle that was flanked on each side by row after row of three-tiered bunks of slatted wood, which were supported by wooden posts maybe ten or twelve feet apart. There were probably at least half a dozen sections on each side of the aisle. Every section housed approximately ten women between the posts on each tier. Mother and I found a little bit of space on the lowest tier and scooted in on our behinds. Others from our group were doing the same thing. There was barely enough space to sit without hitting your head on the tier above, and it wasn't deep enough to lie down and stretch your legs. There was a thin plywood wall where the headboard should have been, separating our heads from the women on the other side from us.

Too exhausted to care, I curled up against my mother and fell into a semiconscious sleep. We were all doing the same thing. Body against body, cramped against each other, we lay on the wooden slats until someone said, "Go get your soup." I don't remember how we got them, but we each had a little tin container. We were in a long, single-file line that moved quickly towards a woman who stood by a metal garbage can full of liquid. You stopped for a second as she poured one ladle of what was called "soup" into your container. Food at last! I could hardly wait! I looked into my container and saw two little potato cubes and maybe a one-inch piece of cabbage floating around in grayish water. That was the first bite of food I'd had in four days. We walked back with our precious soup to the bunks, then sat down and ate it, wondering, *What next?* We soon found out: another *Apel*. That was the name for our roll call, standing at attention to be counted. This time we were part of the Auschwitz population, and the counting took a very long time. I think that it was three or four hours, although not having a watch or clock I cannot say for certain. After the count we went back to the barracks to face the long night. Thus ended my first day in Auschwitz.

Our daily routine consisted of: wake-up call at four-thirty AM; stand in line to get our one cup of lukewarm ersatz coffee and a miniscule slice of black bread; go outside for the first three-or-four-hour *Apel*; go back to our building; sit in our allotted spots; and wait. Every day we had another roundup. We'd be marched to a field, told to remove our clothes, and then one by one had to walk in front of a selection committee. Some women were sent to the right and others to the left. The women who went left were never seen again. The rest of us went back to our building, got our bowl of soup later in the day, and afterwards went for the second three-or-four-hour *Apel*.

One cold and dreary morning we saw dead bodies hanging in full sight of our gathering space as we went for the *Apel*. Some inmates had tried to escape. They had been caught and hung. The hanging dead bodies were left on display for a few days, serving as a constant warning of what would happen to every one of us if we should be foolish enough to try such a thing. This type of intimidation seemed to have the desired effect. Wanting to live and survive at any cost was our number-one goal. The Soviet army was pushing forward, and we believed that the Russians were winning and the Germans were in retreat. Soon, soon, they would liberate us. In the tight space of our lower bunk, whispered conversations revolved around two things: survival and the eternal hope of finding a loved one after liberation. We existed one minute, one hour, one day at a time. Passing another inspection was an accomplishment, accompanied by a feeling of triumph.

This routine continued for days on end. A week or so after our arrival in Auschwitz, I developed a severe case of diarrhea, which was prevalent in our group of inmates. Many times I lost control before making it to the "toilet," which was actually just an outdoor ditch covered with a wooden board that had hundreds of cutout holes. During one of the selections my backside and legs were covered with my own feces and mud. I was sent to the "wrong" side, Mother having already passed to the "right" side. We had been separated.

Convinced that I was going to the gas chamber, I trudged along with the other unlucky ones. I hoped that Mother had gone back to our barracks. We walked for a very long time before entering a totally different compound and being informed that we were in *Lager* C. Amazingly, it was not the gas chamber! As soon as I realized that I was not yet going to be murdered, I became totally devastated at the separation from my mother. My primary concern was her survival without me. Somehow I had become the strong one, but together we were a team, bolstering each other's spirits and keeping up our sense of humor. When things were unbearable we found something ridiculous in every situation. We joked about our appearances, sleeping facilities, and "gourmet" food.

Now, for the first time in my life, I was totally alone. I knew that Mother had passed the selection, because she had been sent to join the healthier-looking group of women. The big question was, where? Did she go back to our barracks, or was she in a new place, just as I was? No matter what, I had to find her. With great caution I approached our *Kapo*.

Kapos were inmates, favored by the guards, who were put in charge of us and who did all the dirty work for the Germans, including kicking us, beating us, and doing everything else that the Germans felt was necessary to keep order. Almost all the *Kapos* I came in contact with were mistresses of the male guards: they were pretty, still had their own hair, and were warmly dressed. They wore boots and carried whips. Each building had a *Kapo*, and ours had tiny private quarters of her own. Our *Kapo*, a Polish Jewess who had led us to the new camp, wasn't quite as brutal as some, and in a way was actually decent, which gave me the courage to beg for help. She told me that the female German officer was sometimes sympathetic to our plight, and that if I were to fall down in the mud crying and screaming for my mother, the German woman might be willing to help me. She said, "If your mother is still alive, the German officer has the power either to transfer you to your mother's *Lager* or to order a transfer for your mother to this *Lager*. She has done this before." The *Kapo* turned around and walked away from me. I did as she suggested, and fell face down in the mud, crying and screaming.

Nothing happened. Everyone ignored me. I cried and yelled, and eventually became hysterical. I lost control and couldn't stop screaming. This went on for many hours, and ultimately I must have lost all consciousness. When I came to, it was daylight, and I was inside a building surrounded by four women. Just like me, they were from the Łodz ghetto. They told me that we were in an all-Hungarian Jewish female section of Auschwitz, and, as far as they knew, we were the only Polish Jews. When they heard me screaming in Polish, they knew that they had to help me. They waited until the middle of the night, when no one was supposed to be out of the building. Then, under the cover of darkness, they took a chance. Risking their lives, they went out and carried me inside. Fortunately, they were not caught.

I was never reunited with my mother. In fact, the hysterical performance nearly cost me my life. My diarrhea turned into dysentery. I lost all control of my bowels. I was very weak, and could barely stand up; when I did, a foul, odorous liquid poured out of me. My body would not cooperate, and I was losing ground. Every hour seemed worse than the one before. My newly found friends — or, I should say, my guardian angels — would not let me die. They surrounded me at *Apel*, one in front of me, one behind me, and one on each side. Thus, whichever way I fell, one of them would prop me up. They took me outside to a water spigot and washed my backside. The most selfless act of all was at soup time: each one of them gave up one precious piece of potato from her bowl and put it into mine, which meant that I usually had at least five or six bites of potato each day. Amazingly, this little bit of food helped me to get better.

Our building in *Lager* C consisted of four walls and a roof, with a door in the middle of one of the long walls. There were no bunks. We sat and slept on bare earth. The Hungarian *Kapo* was an utter bitch who hated Polish Jews, and most of the Hungarian Jewish inmates shared her views. Totally ostracized, the five of us managed to stay together. Strangely, there were no selections in *Lager* C. We wore the same clothes that were issued to us when we first arrived in Auschwitz, and we did not work. We were dying of disease and starvation.

Weeks — or maybe a couple of months — later, my friends found out about a work transport out of Auschwitz to Germany. They made a group decision to somehow get to the selection site. We knew that it was probably our one chance to get out of Auschwitz alive. Once we reached the selection, we learned that only able-bodied women were being chosen. I was scared out of my wits that my friends would get to go and that I would be rejected. I shared my fear with them, and without hesitation they all said that if I was rejected they would follow me. To this day I don't know how we managed to stay together, nor do I have any real understanding of how this one unbelievable occurrence came about.

I passed the selection along with everyone else in our little group, which the presence of two more Polish Jewish women increased to seven. I was still the youngest. Sometime during that fall, probably while still at Auschwitz, I had reached my fifteenth birthday, but at the time I lived in a void in which dates had no meaning. The next youngest was Basia, age eighteen. Eva was twenty years old, as were the new girls, who kind of stuck to each other and whose names I don't remember. Hinda and Sala were much older, in their early or middle thirties. Hinda, Sala, and Basia had been very active in the Łodz ghetto communist party. Because of their organizational skills and communal attitude they were able to pull us together into a cohesive group with a philosophy of one for all and all for one. It worked. We had made it out of Auschwitz!

Once again I was in a cattle car with probably at least a hundred women, bound for who knows where. This time we were happy to be in a cattle car. We knew that nothing could be worse than Auschwitz.

Return to Auschwitz

When we got to Auschwitz we had already been to the Warsaw ghetto, and then to Treblinka, Majdanek, Belzec, and Sobibor. At each of the killing camps we had dug our soil, stored it in properly marked little burlap sacks, lit memorial candles, and said our prayers. Each experience was emotionally draining and overwhelming.

The Warsaw Ghetto Holocaust Memorial was the site of our first Friday-night service in Poland. The next day we traveled to Treblinka, an hour's ride from Warsaw in the midst of a beautiful forest. The vastness of it overwhelmed us, with its hundreds of boulders bearing the names of cities and towns where Jews once lived and were no more.

Majdanek is so close to the city of Lublin that only a mile separated the city from the death camp. It is well established that the citizens of Lublin were within hearing distance; yet no one paid attention to the killing of hundreds of thousands of Jews. Today Majdanek is a memorial site. It was jarring for us to see, in one part of the grounds, mothers pushing their baby buggies, children playing, and young lovers strolling, as though it were a park; not far away was a dome containing remnants of the bones and ashes of murdered Jews.

We dug our soil from the edges of a swamp below the dome, which was filled with human ash.

Belzec is another killing camp in eastern Poland. Its only purpose was mass murder. Dreary and desolate, hidden in a forest, it has a grouping of individual memorials spread throughout the entire area. On the day that we went there it never stopped raining. We huddled under umbrellas, dug some soil, said the prayers, and left. This camp is one of the saddest places on this earth, definitely not somewhere to linger or to sightsee. It left an indelible impact on my psyche.

Sobibor was made famous by the movie "Escape from Sobibor." Jake, one of the members of our survivor group, had a cousin who took part in the Sobibor uprising, and who was one of the inmates who killed some Germans. There were almost no survivors from that uprising; except for those few who managed to escape, all the human beings who were transported to Sobibor were murdered. We were there on a very dark and rainy day. As we gathered our soil, lit candles, and recited the prayer for the dead, the earth itself seemed to be crying.

Next on the agenda was our trip to Krakow, where we would spend two nights. This would be our base for the visit to Auschwitz. Krakow is a beautiful and historic city. We stayed in what used to be — and has again become — the Jewish section. There are kosher hotels, kosher Yiddish night clubs, restored old synagogues, and a population of approximately a hundred elderly Jewish survivors of the Holocaust. The place has an eerie atmosphere, with everything to attract Jewish tourists, but with Polish Catholics providing the entertainment. Belting out familiar Yiddish melodies, the young Polish performers do their best to bring back memories of the era before Hitler.

After checking in at the Esther Hotel, we met with two local women survivors who were close to my age. They were not familiar with our story and assumed that we were on a mission for JOINT, a Jewish organization that provides help to needy Jews around the world, particularly to Euro-

pean Holocaust survivors. They related to us their stories of hiding and of passing as Polish Catholics throughout the length of the war. As we became better acquainted, and as they learned that seven of us were also Holocaust survivors, the atmosphere changed. Suddenly we were no longer visiting American Jews but their soulmates. For me, it was an emotionally charged experience.

The next morning our group met for breakfast prior to our tour of the city and our trip to Auschwitz. My body has never forgotten the five years of starvation, and any association with the Holocaust makes me extremely hungry. I ate a very hearty breakfast. After breakfast we toured the old Jewish section of Krakow. We visited two magnificent synagogues that were undergoing repair and restoration. With music playing in the background, images from yesteryear moved across a video screen.

We also visited a very old Jewish cemetery, where, as luck would have it, we encountered a group of Hasidic American male tourists. This particular sect of Judaism does not accept women as equals, and they were outraged at our presence: we were polluting their space. Our male rabbi tried to talk to them and to explain who we were, but they could not have cared less. We ignored them and stayed. This encounter brought back many unpleasant memories of the Łodz ghetto, where I and my friends had been kicked, pushed, and shoved by people who looked just like these tourists. When it came to procuring food in the ghetto, such men always acted superior to the rest of us — and especially to the children, since they knew that we were physically unable to fight them for our place in the food lines. We responded by kicking back at them. Now the presence and behavior of these Hasidic men at the cemetery spoiled that visit for me, and I was anxious to get away from them.

The tension was mounting as our time to depart for Auschwitz grew nearer. We made one last stop in an old-fashioned Krakow square full of food vendors and souvenir shops. I bought dolls in native costumes, a couple of others purchased fresh fruit, and my daughter Helena showed up at the bus with a huge armload of light-purple lilacs. She was taking them to Auschwitz to honor the memory of everyone who was murdered there. This was a coincidence: Helena had no idea that my mother, her grandmother Ruta, had adored lilacs. From the first bloom till the very end of the lilac season, our home in Poland was filled with huge bouquets of the fragrant flowers. And now Helena was taking lilacs to Auschwitz to meet the ghost of her murdered grandmother. I was too choked up to say anything, but tried to maintain a calm exterior.

I was not prepared for the throng of tourists at Auschwitz, hundreds of people wandering around the place—with special guides, speaking in many languages, leading groups of people around and telling them the story of the camp. One of those guides was appointed for us. As she went into her memorized speech, we interrupted her, saying, "Yes, we know. We were here. We are survivors." Nothing stopped her. Her only reaction to us was impatience at our interruptions. Our own guide, Wloclaw, was not permitted to do a presentation. He begged our patience and promised that he would shortly be in charge again.

After viewing the displays of human hair, the thousands of shoes, and all the other grim reminders of Nazi atrocities, we went to look at a map of Auschwitz. The part of the camp that I had been in was Auschwitz II, also known as Birkenau. Within Birkenau there were three sectors, and barbed-wire fences further cordoned each of those sectors into smaller camps, or "Lagers." I had been in Lager A with my mother until the point where we were separated, and after that I found myself in Lager C. Lager A was in Sector I; officially Birkenau Ia, it was also known as the "women's camp." What I had known as Lager C was in Sector II. Officially Birkenau IIc, it had originally been a camp for Jews from Hungary. By 1944 it was a camp for Hungarian women, as I had been informed when I arrived there. At that point in the war the Germans' system was beginning to deteriorate, which explains how I and my fellow Poles ended up in Lager C.

We spent many sad hours in our visit to Birkenau. Unlike our experience at the main camp, Auschwitz I, we encountered only one or two couples during the whole time we were there. It was a day like no other. For the first time in my life I saw the vastness of the place. As a slave I had seen only the areas around my barracks, but now we walked for hours and hours. We went to the shower building and to the ruins of the crematoria, where each one of us carefully placed some of Helena's lilacs. We dug soil from a putrid pond directly across from one of the crematoria. The emotional stress left us barely functional.

It was dark by the time we left the area. This was the only camp where we chose to light our candles outside the gates. As soon as we lined up the candles in a sheltered spot, an eerie wind howled all around us as though the spirits were talking to us. Maybe it was the place and the stress of the entire day, but when it was my turn to light a candle I felt hysterical. It seemed as though my mother's spirit was beckoning to me, and I wanted to put my arms around the flame.

Each one of us said a few words. Then we boarded our bus and went back to Krakow.

That night we had dinner reservations at a "Jewish" night club. We went to our rooms, cleaned up, and proceeded to the club to try to change our mood by eating and drinking and making merry. A beautiful blonde was belting out Yiddish songs, and despite our heavy day we managed to enjoy the evening. Yes, we were traumatized. Yet we were celebrating the fact that some of us survived, went on to have children and enjoy a good life! Hitler did not win.

The following morning we departed from Krakow. Łodz was our next destination, and from there it was on to Chelmno, which is located within approximately fifteen miles of each of the towns I had lived in. It is almost like the center of a wheel, with spokes radiating toward Sompolno, Radziejow, and Lubraniec. Chelmno is in the countryside, surrounded by forest on three sides; the setting is lovely and serene, and is somewhat reminiscent of the meadow in Washington Park at the site of our Oregon Holocaust Memorial.

It takes a few minutes for the horror of the place to begin to sink in. Row upon row of raised mounds cover the landscape of an area as big as maybe two or three football fields. These mounds hold ashes and small bits of the bones of Jews who were murdered here. Chelmno was another of the six camps that were built strictly for the purpose of exterminating human beings. Both sets of my grandparents and most of the members of my father's extended family were gassed to death in this place.

For the final time, we dug the soil and ashes, lit candles, and recited prayers. We had completed our mission.

Our last stop was in a lovely meadow with no gruesome memories. We sat in a circle, debriefed, and went through a cleansing ritual. Afterward, we sang songs and returned to the living.

Chapter Six

BERGEN-BELSEN

1944–1945

Another long imprisonment in a cattle car. The conditions were the same as on our trip to Auschwitz: a hundred or so bodies packed like sardines without food, water, or toilet facilities. We pushed and shoved each other, every woman fighting against all odds to sit against a wall of the car. Being part of a cohesive group, my friends and I managed to save enough space for all of us to be next to a wall. Through the sheer desire to survive for just another day, each of us found some vicious inner strength to push and kick anyone who encroached on our personal space.

Yet hope bloomed even under those circumstances. We were out of Auschwitz and on the way to Germany, hopefully to a real labor camp, without gas chambers. This glimmer of hope was enough to keep me going, but I desperately wished that my mother could have been with me. The thought that for sure we would now never find each other was too much to bear.

At last, after three days and nights, the train stopped, and I recognized the familiar sound of someone on the outside unlocking the door of our cattle car. Weak and exhausted, I obediently managed to jump out of the car into a void of darkness. We had arrived in the middle of the night, and to my amazement were in the heart of a forest. Within minutes, the Germans lined us up into a proper marching group. We trudged along a narrow dirt trail that was almost hidden among huge trees and dense undergrowth. Putting one foot in front of the other, I stumbled along with the other women for what seemed like eternity. By daybreak we had reached our destination. We entered a very large, secluded compound, hidden in the midst of the forest.

Although ready to collapse, we had to follow the familiar routine of standing at attention in precise rows and being counted. After the count we were informed that we had arrived in the Bergen-Belsen concentration camp. We stood in line, and each of us received a neatly folded blanket. I couldn't believe my eyes: a real, honest-to-goodness blanket. What luxury! This was definitely going to be a big improvement over Auschwitz. After this we were marched to a huge canvas tent. This tent was our new home.

Hundreds of women entered through the single flap opening. Again an unexpected sight: the ground was covered with fresh straw. We were the first group to occupy this dwelling. Quickly Hinda and Basia walked away from the opening toward the center of the tent, and the rest of us followed them. We gathered as much of the straw as we could grab before anyone else had a chance to get it, and created a large sort of bed, surrounded by the damp, cold earth. The exposed dirt gave us a walkway as well as a barrier between us and the other inmates. The others saw the advantage that we as a group had over a single person and many of them opted to imitate us, so that soon there were a whole bunch of communes. Our group combined all of our blankets, using two or three to cover the straw and the rest as a single joined cover. Now we had a home. The weather was already very cold and this arrangement kept us from freezing to death. We slept curled into each other, and if anyone wanted to change her position we all had to shift in the same direction; in order for us to turn over the whole group had to move in unison. During the day we sat on our mound, and at night we kept a little bit warmer from each others' body heat.

Hinda and Basia were our undisputed leaders. Both of them had been very active in the leadership of the Łodz ghetto communist party, and they organized us in accordance with those principles. Mandatory rule number one: no matter how difficult, we had to keep our bodies clean, hoping to prevent disease. In freezing and foul weather, the seven of us walked daily past the German lookout posts to take our showers. As we passed the guards we took great pleasure in singing patriotic Polish songs. The German guards did not understand our language; to them we sounded like a jolly group of inmates, and they ignored us. This was our way of showing rebellion without being caught.

The shower consisted of a tall water pipe with an attached sieve pointing downward. It was out in the open, in clear view of the guards in the lookout towers. I remember taking off my little Auschwitz dress, laying it on the ground just far enough from the shower head to keep it dry, and then standing under the stinging, ice-cold spray of water, hoping to remove some of the grime and lice from my body. The temperature must have been in the teens or twenties and yet the lice managed to survive and multiply. No matter how hard we tried, it was impossible to get rid of them. Despite the freezing temperature and the proliferation of lice we followed this daily ritual. It gave us a feeling of empowerment and made us feel somewhat more human.

In Bergen-Belsen, disease and malnutrition were our greatest enemies. It was fairly safe to walk around the camp. There were no gas chambers. We still had to stand twice daily to be counted. We had selections, but, instead of being sent to the gas chamber, women were selected for factory work in German cities. Thousands of us, though, died from disease and starvation. Knowing that disease was carried by the lice, our little group tried to protect itself by taking our mandatory daily showers. Every few days one of us showered in whatever she was wearing, just to try to clean some lice out of her filthy garment. We would wrap that girl in a blanket until we had to go out for the lineup. After returning from the lineup she would again be wrapped in a blanket. Somehow we managed to keep this up without being punished.

Starvation was impossible to combat. There was no food beyond the single cup of ersatz coffee and half slice of bread in the morning, and in the evening a small bowl of soup. This "soup" consisted of gray water with a couple of cubes of potato, an occasional potato peel, or a piece of cabbage or kohlrabi floating in it. We never had potato, potato skins, cabbage, and kohlrabi at the same time; mostly it was one or possibly two of these items. Each tiny, bite-size morsel was more valuable than the biggest diamond. It literally made the difference between life and death.

Every morning and evening our *Kapo* selected two women to fetch the food — the bread, along with a garbage can full of coffee in the morning and a container of soup the same size in the evening. She asked for volunteers, but very few inmates wanted to attempt the long walk to fetch the soup. It was a physically demanding job to bring back the heavy can, on a path that was usually icy and slippery. The contents of this single can fed hundreds of women; it probably weighed as much as one of us did, and it had always to be lifted above the ground, not dragged. In our emaciated condition it took a heroic effort to execute this task. The foremost question was whether you were strong enough to schlep the heavy container to its destination.

As a group we decided to have at least one and preferably two of us volunteer for this task as often as possible. There was a reward for doing this. The *Kapo*, in dishing out the soup, would dig deep down into the bottom of the can where the goodies were and come up with a ladle full of potatoes or other solid items for the first two bowls, which went to the two soup carriers. In accordance with good communal living, our group would then count out every piece of potato in all of our bowls, divide the total by seven, and evenly redistribute the contents. There was one caveat: if any one of us was getting weaker, or sick, the rest of us each gave up one piece of potato to the sick one. It was the same concept that they had used to snap me out of the jaws of death in Auschwitz. Our method seemed to work, since all seven of us managed to stay in relatively decent health.

A few weeks after our arrival in Bergen-Belsen, a second tent rose on the horizon. We were within walking distance and could see that it housed another transport of women. Soon everyone was talking about them. They came from Auschwitz *Lager* A, and when I heard that my hopes soared. That had been our original *Lager*, and my mother had been sent back to it at our separation. Maybe, maybe my mother was in this group. Without saying a word to my friends, I took off at a run to find her. Throngs of emaciated women with empty, staring eyes were milling around. My heart pounding with fear and hope, I approached one of these groups. I was crying and yelling her name, asking whether anyone knew Ruta Kominkowska. No one responded. Expressionless faces looked through me as though I was invisible. I did not recognise a single person. Asking if there was anyone from the last Łodz transport to Auschwitz, I was met by indifference and total silence. I went from group to group, crying, begging, pleading, "Talk to me!" Still no response. No one recognized me and I didn't see a single familiar face. Even if my mother wasn't in this transport, I still had hope that maybe someone had known her in Auschwitz. All I needed was to know that she was still alive and that I could continue to live with hope of her survival.

After a couple of hours I saw, somewhat isolated from the other inmates, two women sitting together who were actually looking at me. I carefully approached them and started a conversation. They were sisters and seemed to feel sufficient unto themselves. They said they were originally from the Łodz ghetto. I could barely contain myself. An inner voice said, *Be careful. Don't spook them.* Gingerly carrying on a general conversation, I led up to a casual question. "Did you know a Ruta Kominkowska?" They looked at each other and one of them said to her sister, "Wasn't that the name of the fancy lady in the ghetto?" "Oh, that one. Remember, she was crazy, running around in Auschwitz screaming a name. They said she was looking for her daughter." "I bet you that they took her to the gas chambers. She must be dead by now." They wanted to know why I was interested in her whereabouts. When I told them that she was my mother, they stopped talking and turned away from me. Knowing that it was useless to try and pursue more conversation with them, I walked away and went back to our tent.

I never mentioned this experience to anyone in our little group. Something changed in me on that day. My will to live turned into steel. I had to survive to avenge my whole family and to carry on the memory of my parents and grandparents. I was either fourteen or fifteen. My birthday was on October 21st, but I knew not what day or month it was, only that it was either winter or late fall, and very cold. Maybe I had turned fifteen in Auschwitz; maybe I was still fourteen. It didn't matter, I was now the only survivor of my immediate family. I had to live, to have children, to carry the family forward. My children would be named after my parents and grandparents. I was determined to live, and by doing so to achieve a personal triumph over the Nazis. I didn't know how I would accomplish this miracle. I taught myself to live and to focus only on the future and liberation. The Americans would come and set me free. I would contact Uncle Moniek in America and he would help me. I dreamt of a life full of love and laughter, of a house full of children, but, most of all, of a life free of starvation and deprivation.

And so I returned to my tent in silence, and settled in on our pile of straw and blankets. Somehow my change must have been noticed by Basia because she began to include me in the decision-making process. It made me feel like an important member of our group. Hinda and Basia were our leaders, and they had chosen me, the youngest in our group, to participate in decisions that affected all of us.

Without warning, extremely severe winter weather was upon us. It snowed nonstop for days at a time, covering the frozen ground with a heavy blanket of snow. Eventually we had snowdrifts up to three feet high, but nothing stopped the daily routine of being forced to stand at attention and be counted. We were still clad only in our one piece of

Auschwitz clothing, with no underwear, and with no socks in our ill-fitting and mismatched shoes. My feet were perpetually red and swollen, and I couldn't feel my toes. Without exception, we were all suffering from frostbite. Our hair was not growing back, and bare, shaved heads, covered with layers of snow, were a normal sight. Somehow we managed to stand at attention without fainting or falling down until the ordeal was over; then we stumbled back to our tent until the next time, which was only a night or a few daylight hours away. In between we sat inside and talked.

Desperate to survive the cold, we came up with a very dangerous idea. We would unravel one of the blankets and knit some socks and underwear. Since I was a very fast and adept knitter, it was my job to fashion those garments. There were no knitting needles, but, living in the forest as we were, we found a few twigs that I could use as a substitute. The unraveled blanket was hidden between the other blankets and everyone was on the lookout for the *Kapo* or a German. The moment we sensed danger, everything would be hidden between the blankets. In no time at all I had produced something that looked like socks and underpants, the latter with a string of wool pulled through the top so that they would stay on. We wore the underpants all the time, even while standing outside for the count. The socks were visible and were therefore worn only when we came inside. We were never caught, and probably owed our survival to the little bit of extra warmth that these items gave us. Fortunately, no one reported us to the *Kapo*, and soon many of the other women followed our example. Many blankets mysteriously disappeared in our tent. This act of deception and defiance boosted our morale. It felt great to outmaneuver the Germans.

With nothing else to do, we sat on our bed and talked nonstop about the future. Our discussions continued for hours, as we sat there killing lice between our thumbnails, picking them off of each other as well as from our own clothing. They were plump and juicy, and their blood squirted all over our hands as we continued our conversations.

On one such day the subject was: "Where will you go after the liberation?" I shared with them my dream of going to America to be with Uncle Moniek and his wife. He had left Poland in 1938, but I knew him well, since he was my mother's younger brother and only sibling. Sala said, "I have a cousin in America." "Oh," said I, "My uncle lives in Portland, Oregon. He went there to marry his American sweetheart." Sala replied, "My cousin also lives in Portland, Oregon, and I met her once when she and her mother were on a grand tour of Europe and came to Isbica to meet some of their family." My uncle had met Ciocia Hanita when she was on a grand tour of Europe and visited family in Aleksandrow, Kujawski. Sala continued, "My cousin's name is Hanita Asher." I exclaimed, "My uncle married Hanita Asher!" We looked at each other in total amazement. We had a link from the past. My goodness, we were practically family. Once we got used to seeing each other from this new perspective, we chattered on like a couple of magpies.

I filled her in on this most unlikely romance, which had ensued after just a few hours of the two being together. Hanita spoke only English, while my uncle, though he was multilingual and spoke German, French, Polish, and Yiddish, did not speak English. Even so, they had somehow managed to communicate. From that time on they corresponded, and he tried to get out of Poland to America. It took him more than four years to accomplish his goal. I had just turned nine when he left, and had not seen him since the evening in November when he kissed me goodbye. My father escorted him to Warsaw and then on to Gdynia, where he boarded a ship bound for the United States.

I told Sala how I had memorized his address and repeated it to myself every night. After the war I was going to write to him. She thought that I was doing the right thing and said that she might also write to her cousin, my aunt Hanita, after the war.

Suddenly one day we heard that German factory executives were in camp, selecting women for transport to work as slave laborers in their factories. By late that afternoon, our *Kapo* came in, yelling, "Get outside! Line up! We are having a work selection!" After quite a few hours of standing at attention, we were approached by a German civilian escorted by some SS, or perhaps merely by some camp guards — I never knew who was who — who proceeded to inspect us. The civilian would stop in front of a woman and look her over, and then he either continued walking or had the woman step out of line and go to another holding area. Not knowing what it all meant, our little group stood together in the lineup.

The German civilian certainly took his time, and the very slow and methodical process took its toll on our emotions. Not sure of what to hope for, whether it would be best to stay or to be sent to the other area, we had only one desire: to stay together. Luck was with us. He selected all seven of us for the holding area.

After this selection was complete, we were lined up and marched out of the camp. It was probably early evening, and darkness engulfed us. Following the same path that had brought us to the camp, we marched in complete silence. The temperature had been warming, and the ice and snow had partially melted into a sea of muck. Without warning, I stepped into a rut in the road that twisted my foot. I felt an incredible piercing object wedge itself into my left ankle as I stumbled and fell to my knees. An uncontrollable groan of pain escaped from my lips. Instantly one of my friends was at my side, telling me to be quiet, get up, and start walking. "If you don't get up and walk they will kill you!" Knowing that she was right, I stifled a half-formed scream, got up, and somehow marched on, keeping pace with the other women.

By the time we reached the train I could barely stand. I had no strength left to climb into the cattle car. Someone was pushing me up and a couple of arms dragged me inside. My foot was throbbing, hot, and very swollen. I tried to stretch it out in front of me, with an immediate reaction from a woman I did not know. She hit my leg, and as I screamed in agony and pulled it back, she told me that I had encroached on her space and I had better not do it again. My friends came to my rescue, turning my body so that my leg could be stretched across them. It was the middle of the night and the inside of our cattle car was pitch-black. My friends felt my foot, and found what they thought was a nail embedded all the way to its head just under my ankle. One of them held me down as another tried to pull it out. With bare fingers she tried to get ahold of the nailhead. I screamed and she pulled, and at last she got a good grip and managed to yank it out. It wasn't just a nail. She had removed a rusty screw, fairly thick and an inch long, from my foot.

After that my memory is fuzzy. I know that the wound was full of pus, and that I ran a very high fever throughout the two-or-three-day trip. By the time the train stopped I was lucid, and a thick, pus-filled scar had grown over the hole. My ankle was still very sore, but I knew that I would persevere and that I would make it.

We had arrived in a German city. I managed to jump out of the car and marched with the whole group to a labor camp that was to be our next home. We were in Magdeburg, Germany.

After years of confinement in the Łodz ghetto, Auschwitz, and Bergen-Belsen, it seemed somewhat unreal to be marching in the middle of the road in a real city. We had arrived at daybreak. Most of the residents were still asleep, and the few who were walking on the sidewalks did not react to our presence; we were just part of their normal, everyday scenery. Eventually we arrived at our destination.

To my surprise, this camp had paved roads and sidewalks lined with rows of neat-looking wooden buildings with real doors and windows. One of these was where we would live. The first thing I noticed was an actual wooden floor. Rows of communal three-level bunks occupied every inch of interior space. Each level had a solid wooden base and some blankets. I vaguely remember a few inches of straw covering the boards.

My friends and I quickly found and claimed our sleeping territory, settling in on the top tier. This was not as desirable to everyone because of having to climb up there. We didn't mind, though, and we were happy to have a little bit more head room. I managed to spread out and ease the pain in my throbbing foot.

A few hours later, we stood outside our building in the usual, neat, perfectly formed rows. This time we were being selected for slave labor. Numerous factory representatives came to the camp to pick and choose their laborers. Knowing that they could work us to death and then return to the camp and get more slaves, they were not too picky. We were all replaceable and expendable.

I was selected by a tall, angular, German woman, who looked very grim and ominous. My friends had been chosen by other people, and I was scared. I went where I was told and stood with a couple of very slight girls. As I watched, the woman chose only the smallest and skinniest from the lineup. My heart sank. This looked dangerously hopeless. I was sure that my luck had run out, and that this group was being selected for extermination. I can't remember how many she chose, but there were fewer than ten of us. The selection ended and we were sent back to our barracks. Early the next morning the supervisor of our building called our names. She took us to a designated holding area, where we waited for the German woman to come get us and lead us to our unknown fate.

One more time we marched through the sleeping city. Thoughts scrambled around in my head as I steadily trudged along. *Is this the end for me?* Yet, through the months of conditioning, I saw no means of escape if I tried to run away. I felt more protected and less vulnerable as part of a group, and totally accepted our collective fate, thinking that it was safer to march with the group than to try to run away and be instantly shot and killed. At least I was still alive, and maybe we would all be spared. These thoughts kept me moving.

Our little band of skeletons marched on. Not a word was spoken. At last we reached a gated area, with German guards posted at the entrance. The woman said something to them and they let us in. We entered a building and she led us through a labyrinth of hallways, turning right and left, up and down stairs, until we reached a room. At one end of the room was a door. We were ordered to go through the door and found ourselves in a large closet. A fleeting thought — *Is this a gas chamber?* — entered my mind. Cautiously I looked around. The space was lit by a single electric bulb dangling from the ceiling. I noticed a few stools, some sacks of potatoes, tin buckets. Some of the buckets were filled with water and a few were empty. The woman was explaining our job to us. Not yelling, just talking in a normal tone of voice, she let us know that we were in a factory dining area for German guards and employees. We were to peel all the potatoes. The potato peels should go into the empty buckets, and the peeled potatoes into the buckets of water. We were to work quickly and keep the peel very thin. She told us that we would be watched through a peephole, and that if we got caught eating we would be severely punished and sent back to the labor camp. She left our tiny work area and locked us in from the outside.

I couldn't believe my luck. To be peeling potatoes in a warm room was as close to heaven as I had known in a very long time. We knew that we shouldn't eat anything, but each of us managed to sneak a bite of potato peel. A couple of hours had passed when I heard a key turning in the lock. Struck with fear, I knew that we had been caught. The same German woman entered. She shut the door behind her and leaned her back against it, obstructing the peephole into our closet. She was wearing the same long cape that she had worn in the morning while marching us to work. Silently she put a finger to her lips, indicating for us to be quiet. In a low whisper, she proceeded to tell us, "I couldn't talk to you on the street or in the camp, and I have to be very careful not to get caught. I want you to know that I selected all of you because you are the smallest and youngest in the transport and I want to help you survive. On my arm, under the cape, is a pot of hot soup from the kitchen. It is for you. Please listen to me and be very careful. I will place the pot against the door; that way no one can see it through the peephole. Carefully, one at a time, try as casually as you can to have a reason for moving about this room. When you're close enough to the door and can't be seen, take a few bites of soup and move quietly away from the door. There is enough for all of you, so take your time. I have the only key to this room, and no one can walk in on you. I will return for the pot." This whole process must have taken less than a minute. Unaccustomed to kindness, I found this act almost beyond comprehension. She continued to bring us some food on a daily basis. She brought us rainwear for our daily march, and once she even took us to her residence for some cookies and hot tea. I never knew her name.

One morning, maybe a week or so into this experience, I woke up and couldn't stand. My legs buckled. I could not move my head, and was burning up with fever. My friends covered me with blankets and made up the bed over me. They were satisfied with the way it all looked and told me not to move or make a sound while they were gone. I was in agony and spent most of that day sleeping, without being discovered. When my friends returned from work they took one look at me and burst out laughing. Evidently my face and neck were very swollen and I looked like a chipmunk. I had the mumps! They hid me for three more days. I slept for most of the time, until the fever began to break.

During inspection on the fourth morning I must have moved or made a sound, because the building supervisor found me. Immediately she made me get up, and as punishment sent me outside to carry buckets of coal. Each bucket must have weighed thirty pounds. I was instructed to fill a bucket with coal, carry it to a designated spot, empty it, and start over again. Barely even able to stand up, I nevertheless did as ordered. Slipping and sliding on the icy sidewalk, I trudged back and forth until I reached a point where I just couldn't lift the bucket, so I dragged it on the ground. Stumbling and falling, I knew that I would not last through the day. On the other side of the street, a middle-aged, somewhat obese SS was observing my struggle. Suddenly he crossed the street and walked toward me, as once again I fell to the ground. I helplessly waited for him to shoot me. I saw the black boots and just gave up hope. Then I heard his voice, which was gentle as he asked me, "How old are you? Why are you carrying this heavy bucket of coal?" I answered in proper German. He made me leave the bucket on the sidewalk and walked me to my building. Once we got there, he sent me to lie down and told our *Kapo* to leave me alone. She groveled before him and promised that I would rest for the remainder of the day.

The next day I went back to peeling potatoes, and I continued to work there in the peeling closet for a couple of weeks. One day, though, we were given chest X-rays to screen us for tuberculosis. A few days later our German woman came to the closet, accompanied by a man, and they called my name. I was informed that my X-ray showed that I had the dreaded disease and could no longer work in the kitchen. The man escorted me directly to the "hospital" at the work camp.

I was put into a tiny room with a Russian, a Gypsy, and a Hungarian. The Russian woman and the Gypsy understood each other, and I could speak with the Russian, since she spoke some broken German. We all used sign language, and somehow we got along. The Gypsy wanted to read my hand. The Russian translated what the Gypsy was saying. It was eerie: the Gypsy saw a long lifeline and a ship on a huge sea, and predicted a long sea voyage in my future.

A couple of times my friends were able to visit me. After several days an SS female came in, called my name, and took me out of the camp. We stopped to pick up another Polish Jewish woman and walked to a train station. The three of us boarded an empty passenger car. When the train reached our destination we disembarked and I found myself back in Bergen-Belsen. There the SS woman turned us over to a guard and left.

The other woman's name was Edzia. She was much older than I. We did not become close friends but found it prudent to stick together. I had never seen this part of the camp. No tents, just buildings identical to the ones in Auschwitz, and the same triple bunks, with a divider and with women on the other side of it. We could not see each other, and it sounded like bedlam. So many languages. I remember us trying to identify ourselves by our nationality to the other invisible inmates, melodic voices calling out in Italian, French, Hungarian, Dutch, and Greek, and our response: "We are Polish."

We were starving, filthy, and lice-infested. There was no work, no food, just filth and disease. We were constantly being moved from building to building, and eventually Edzia and I found ourselves in a place with no floors or bunks. We just sat and slept on bare ground. We still got a tiny piece of bread, the cup of ersatz coffee, and, at the end of the day, the soup. Some of us ate a couple of bites of bread in the morning and saved the rest for evening. That piece of bread had to be hidden carefully and guarded. Falling asleep was dangerous, because another woman would do anything to get it away from you. Edzia and I took turns guarding our bread.

We had a Hungarian *Kapo* who carried a whip and wasn't afraid to use it. She was vile, making our life even worse than it already was. She had beautiful, long, red hair, dressed well, and looked well fed. She was one of the Gestapo whores. There were many of them, all Jewesses, yet they did most of the beating and abusive torture for the Germans. One day our *Kapo* came in with a German female officer, asking if any of us was a seamstress. Edzia had been a professional seamstress before the war, but was afraid to respond, not knowing what it meant. At last she took a chance and raised her hand. She was told to follow them. I did not see her for most of that day, and was getting quite concerned when she suddenly showed up. It was an incredible story. The German woman wanted a private seamstress and Edzia filled the bill. She had passed the sewing assignment with flying colors, and the woman was coming back for her in the morning. She told me that all day long she sat at a sewing machine in a warm room. She was also given food. What luck! Edzia offered me half of her slice of bread in return for guarding it while she was gone.

This worked for both of us. I now had two more bites of bread. The other women almost killed me trying to get at it. But, despite the extra two bites, I was getting weaker and sick. At last I realized that I had typhus. Feverish and disoriented, I valiantly kept hanging on to life. Dancing images of my father looked down at me from way up high in the sky. He talked to me, always the same message: "Sweetheart, you are going to live." His sad blue eyes held so much pain, yet he kept smiling at me. I remember my parched lips whispering, "I will, Daddy. I will."

They continued to move us from one building to another, dead bodies piled up outside, frozen into huge human haystacks. With so many people dying, there were fewer and fewer of us, and as the population dwindled they would consolidate two or three buildings into one.

My last clear memory is of Edzia and a few other healthier women at our final move, commandeering what had been the German officers' bathroom. They barricaded themselves inside and locked the door. I wasn't allowed to join them. Even though I begged and pleaded, they would not let me in because I was sick. I found a tiny spot between some strangers and collapsed. Banshee-like screams woke me out of my stupor. I was next to a woman and her two daughters. As they were telling her to let go and die she kept on screaming. They tried to make her more comfortable and lifted her slightly. I saw a pool of blood and a pile of her intestines on the ground beneath her.

Not being able to stand up, I crawled away and found another spot of ground as far away from them as I could. This accomplished, I blacked out. No one came near us. We were the untouchables. This was the final dying place for the typhus people. No food — not even a drop of water — was available to us. I remember floating and hallucinating, coming to for a few minutes, and going under. It might have been a week or maybe more before my fever broke and lucidity returned. Now I was in a more peaceful sleep.

At last I was aware of my surroundings. I tried to move my arms but could not. Something heavy had me pinned down and I did not have the strength to move out from under. It took a long time of tugging, passing out, coming to, and pulling some more, before I managed to free my left arm. We only had about fourteen inches of space per person, and I became aware that the woman on my left was partially sprawled over me. As I tried to push her off, I realized that her body was stiff and cold. It hit me that she was dead. With this knowledge I felt liberated, thinking that now I could lay on top of her. That is exactly what I did, and I immediately fell asleep.

"The Germans are gone! The Germans are gone!" This cry penetrated through my haze. Women — really, just skeletons — were walking outside. But I could not get up. Clawing at the bare earth, I pulled myself on my belly to the opening, where I spotted a cistern a few yards away. The cistern had a spigot, and I knew that I had to get to it and have a drink of water. Pulling my body across this chasm of space was almost an impossible task, but I did it. I drank a few drops of water, and managed to sit up and lean against the rocks.

There I witnessed the most incredible sight. Army trucks were arriving, but they were not German. I thought at first that it was the Americans, but actually they were British. Men had come from the adjoining men's camp, and we had total bedlam. People yelling questions, asking whether there is anyone here from such-and-such town, city, or village. Do you know this person? Do you know that one? All those questions without any answers. I just sat and stared.

Chapter Seven

LIBERATION

1945

Liberation. I didn't know what the word meant. Did the British and American soldiers know about our plight and come to rescue us, or did they accidentally stumble upon the camp while conquering the Germans? Their shocked reaction implied the latter. The one thing that I did understand was that the German guards were gone and we were free. *Free.* What a strange concept. I had no place to go, except to return to the same building. I must have crawled back, because there I was in another spot, away from the dead body. With liberation came more deaths. It was too late for so many, and it seemed that I was one of those. Floating in and out of consciousness, I have vague memories of people lifting my head and trying to feed me. I remember that Edzia came looking for me. She brought me a tiny green onion; the woman next to me tried to steal it and I almost clawed her eyes out. I won the battle, and ate my treasured gift. Despite this burst of strength, my body was too far gone and I collapsed.

Time had no meaning. It might have been hours or days later when I woke up and realized that people were lifting my body and putting me on a stretcher. Panic-stricken, I knew without any doubt that they were taking me to the crematorium. I can still hear my own screams, pleading with them to let me be: "I am OK! Please let me stay! I can work! I'll work for you!" I begged for my life.

"It is OK, little one. We are taking you to the hospital."

"No! No! Not to the hospital! I can work!"

"You're sick. You need medical care."

I had used my last ounce of energy, and succumbed to the black void that enveloped me.

When I woke up, I felt something soft and comfortable underneath me. Slowly I opened my eyes and saw a white cover on my body; everything around me was so soft and white. My first thought was, *I didn't make it. I must have died and now I am floating on clouds.* I saw a woman dressed in a white dress, white shoes, and white stockings, with a white cap on her head. Her appearance affirmed my belief that I was dead; after all, I was looking at an angel! She approached my bed and explained to me that she was a nurse and that I was in a field hospital. They were waiting for me to stabilize, and then they would transfer me to the regular hospital. After that bit of news I must have drifted into another period of lost consciousness.

The next time I came to I was in a bed with guard rails, in yet another place. Identical beds surrounded me. My body couldn't move, but I could turn my head from side to side. Every time I floated back to life, there were different faces in the two beds flanking me on either side. Once I saw a pair of bright-blue eyes looking at me from one of the adjoining beds. To my great surprise, the next time I looked the owner of those eyes was still there. After numerous smiles we both realized that the other was still alive. We exchanged a few words and I blacked out. When I came to I was scared to look, expecting to see a new face, but I was again pleasantly surprised. The owner of the blue eyes was still there. We smiled and started a tentative conversation. Her name was Zosia, and she was also Polish. Zosia was in much better shape than I and was more aware of our circumstances. She told me that we were in a thirty-seven-bed women's death ward. Most of the patients died within one or two days. She and I were exceptions to the rule.

Zosia quickly regained her strength and was moved to a private room. I, on the other hand, was deemed terminal, and had to stay where I was. Zosia visited me at least two or three times a day, assuring me that

I was going to make it and that she intended to pester the doctors until they let her take me to her room. She kept her word. At last the doctors gave in to her and agreed to give me a chest X-ray. Zosia stayed with me till a doctor came back with the results. She had promised that if the X-ray was bad she would stop pestering them. Against all odds, the doctor came in and said, "It's unbelievable, but she doesn't have tuberculosis, just some scar tissue. We'll move her in with you." Within minutes Zosia was pushing my bed to her room. I was so weak that even standing up was out of the question.

She had already made friends with a lot of other Polish survivors in different parts of the sprawling hospital. They all came to my rescue. They would lift me out of bed into a wheelchair and take me outside for some fresh air. It became their mission to save me. I was fifteen and they were all in their twenties, and I was the youngster who would make it. Every one of them had their own horrible story. Zosia had been caught in a Warsaw massacre; she had witnessed her mother's rape; her husband and father were taken for slave labor, she did not know where; and her baby boy was dismembered in front of her eyes. She never talked about where she had been interned prior to Bergen-Belsen. Oh, and, by the way, Zosia and her friends were all Polish Catholics. I was the only Jew in the group, but it made no difference to them. I was a Polish child and they loved me.

They nurtured me back to health. We received Red Cross packages. Among other things, each package held two cigarettes, which were worth a fortune on the black market. Zosia and I did not smoke, so she bartered our cigarettes away, each one worth a pair of eggs. While I was still bedridden, the others went into the forest and picked mushrooms. Zosia taught the foreigners in the kitchen how to cook Polish mushrooms and eggs. We ate buckets of them along with the hospital food.

Zosia was incredible. First she taught me to fall out of bed without killing myself. The next step was huge: I had to stand up on my own. The first time I tried this I collapsed into a heap on the floor, but the next time I held on to the bed and managed to stand for maybe ten seconds. She worked me nonstop until I could take a few steps. After a few weeks I walked like a normal person. The loving care was healing not only my body but also my spirit. I wasn't alone!

One day an English doctor and a translator came to our room. They asked Zosia whether she would like to go to Sweden, telling her that it was a lovely place where she could get good food and continue to recover. She of course said yes. I panicked. I had to go with her. As scared as I was, I remembered a few English words from my past education. Quickly I said, "Doctor, me go Sveden too, please." I remember his sad expression as he told me, in English, "I'm sorry, little one, but we are not taking children." I had reached the end of my ability and could not understand a word. The translator came to our rescue. I replied, "But doctor, I am not a child." He looked at me with those sad eyes and said, "I know, I know. How old are you? Nine, or maybe ten?" "No doctor, I am fifteen." He stared at me in utter horror and disbelief. Tears welled in his eyes. With one tear slowly dribbling down his cheek, he said, mimicking my accent, "Yes, little one. You are going to Sveden."

Shortly thereafter, Zosia, I, and most of our friends were on the way to Lübeck, Germany, from which we would depart for Sweden. This was to be a five-or-six-hour sea voyage, but nothing ever works as planned. A huge storm blew in. Ships were anchored in the harbor, waiting for the weather to improve before they could venture out to sea. We had no place to stay and were taken to a large horse barn, without a floor. The raw earth beneath our feet turned into a sea of muck. The downpour continued for a number of days, and our men became very inventive. They found a few wooden doors stacked against a wall, and leaned them against the troughs on the perimeter of the barn. This created a dry, sloping surface for sleeping, but unfortunately the angle was very steep and we constantly slid down into the mud. After a few days the storm passed, and we boarded a small ship for the crossing to Sweden. It was still raining, but none of us cared. We stood on the deck watching Germany become barely a speck on the horizon. That was the first time I really felt liberated. I was free of Germany!

Our Swedish camp was absolutely wonderful. It had been a health resort, or maybe a summer camp. We were in the town of Ramlösa. Tons of little buildings sat nestled among lovely landscaped grounds full of trees and flowers. Men and women lived separately, with separate communal bathrooms. Residing on the property was one very large building, which housed our dining room, post office, and all the offices for the directors and workers. The dining room held large round tables, and at mealtime the center of each table held huge bowls of boiled potatoes, bread, fish, and other food. I know that I ate a dozen potatoes and probably half a loaf of bread at each meal.

We lived confined in the camp for three weeks of quarantine. Once that ended, we were free to roam the city at our leisure. Many afternoons Zosia, I, and some of our friends went into town. We would buy loaves of bread and cans of sardines, and eat them while sitting on a park bench basking in warm sunshine. We literally inhaled the food, which was only a snack between meals. An hour or two later, we were back at camp eating dinner. It felt as if we could never consume enough food. Once during our forays, probably close to three months after liberation, we found a scale and decided to weigh ourselves. I weighed twenty-five kilograms, roughly fifty-five pounds.

When it was time for us to leave Ramlösa, the staff threw a party in our honor and presented each of us with a little hand-decorated book of national anthems, representing every nationality in our diverse group. I still have this booklet. It begins alphabetically with Austria, continues with Belgium, Czechoslovakia, Holland, Hungary, Italy, Jugoslavia, Lithuania, Poland, and Rumania, and ends with our host country, Sweden. We sang our hearts out. At the end, some of the Jewish people in our group sang "Ha Tikva," and remembering the words and melody I joined in. After the ceremony we departed to different camps throughout Sweden. All of us in the Polish group were transferred to a camp for displaced persons — a "DP" camp — in Hellsingboro.

Even though there were many Jewish survivors there, I had absolutely no contact with them. We lived at opposite ends of the camp. The Jewish group despised and hated the Poles, and spat on the ground whenever they passed us. They had no use for me, because I considered myself Polish. We existed in two different worlds, with mutual distrust and hatred. As for me, I was much more comfortable where I was, and knew that I belonged with my Polish Catholic protectors. Many bad things happened to women in that place. Sexual behavior was rampant and rape was commonplace. My friends protected me, and let it be known that if any man so much as touched me he wouldn't be safe. They would get him.

Immediately after arriving in Sweden I wrote a letter to Uncle Moniek in Portland, Oregon, in the United States of America. Throughout my whole ordeal I had never forgotten his address. Now, day after day, I stood at mail call, waiting for someone to call my name because I had a letter. It never happened. And I read every posted Red Cross list of survivors, but always drew a blank. Not even one familiar name appeared on the lists. I wrote two more letters to my uncle, and again there was no answer. I had been mailing them through the post office on our camp grounds. Out of desperation I decided to write one more time. This time I mailed it through the city post office. Approximately ten days later I was called to the camp director's office. He had a telegram for me, from my uncle: "Thank god you're alive! Letter to follow."

My heart beat wildly as I ran back to our building and ecstatically shared my good news with Zosia. All I could do was to calm down and impatiently wait for the letter!

A few days after receiving the telegram, I was called back to the camp director's office. I was full of hope that my uncle's letter had arrived, but this was not the case. Instead, I was informed by the director that a Swedish gentleman and his wife — the couple had been contacted by a relative of theirs who resided in Portland, Oregon — wanted to come to visit me. In order to do so they would need my consent, which I gave.

My uncle's letter, though, arrived before their visit. Uncle Moniek was almost incoherent in his excitement. He and Aunt Hanita were already making contacts in an effort to get me out of Europe. I was to come and live with them in Portland. They had met with the Swedish consul there, and the people who were coming to meet me were the Larsgards, an aunt and uncle of the consul's wife. There was a possibility that I might be able to live with them.

When I met the strangers, they were much older than I had expected, more the age of my grandparents than of my uncle. He wore a black suit and his shirt had a clerical collar. She was very short and kind of chubby, like my Grandma Helenka. Warm smiles greeted my scared, doubtful look. They seemed very kind, and I immediately felt comfortable with them. Language was not a problem, since both they and I spoke fluent German. After a short visit I was invited to stay with them.

Even though I liked them, they lived in another city. I would have to leave yet another familiar environment and would not be able to see Zosia. This scared me to death. Zosia and the other Polish men and women were my family, and now I would have to leave them. When I mentioned this, the couple immediately told me that I would be able to speak to Zosia on the phone, and that they would also help me with train transportation so that I could visit her every couple of weeks. Feeling better about the situation, I agreed to the move. They would return for me within a few days.

The Larsgards were as good as their word, and before I knew it they had returned to get me. After tearful goodbyes, we left the camp and drove through some beautiful landscapes to their home town of Landskrona. This was to be my new home. I couldn't believe my eyes! The transition from a DP camp to an actual residence was overwhelming. Imagine: a lovely and spacious home. I had not seen anything like it since 1939, when we left our modern apartment in Aleksandrow and moved to Lubraniec. We walked up four flights of stairs and entered their beautiful apartment. The maid was waiting to meet me, and had coffee and treats set out for us. After a few formalities I was taken to my room. I had a private bedroom! It even had private access from the outside hall, and I was given a key! The Larsgards told me that this was my home and that I was free to come and go as I pleased. I had nowhere to go, of course, but it was a nice and thoughtful gesture. Without a word they communicated to me their awareness of my need for freedom.

The Larsgards, who I called Tante Maria and Uncle Nels, had an only daughter, Gudrun, who lived in another city. There was, though, a large extended family in Landskrona. The women were perpetually getting together for afternoon coffee klatches, and I was included in everything they did. They embroidered, knitted, or crocheted nonstop while sipping coffee, eating delicious pastries, and idly chattering away the hours. None of them spoke German, nor, as far as I know, any other foreign language. They knew only Swedish, which was totally foreign to me. We just smiled at each other and drank coffee. Fortunately I could knit, crochet, and embroider, so I fit right in with the elderly ladies. Words will never describe the caring kindness of all those women. After a few visits I learned to say "*Tak, tak*," and "*Tak so mikie*"—"Thank you, thank you," and "Thank you very much."

Zosia and I stayed in touch. I actually visited her once and then she was transferred to another DP camp. One day she called to tell me that she was going home to Poland, and would write to me as soon as she got settled and had an address. I never heard from her. Like all the other important people in my life, she just disappeared.

The Larsgards were wonderful, kind, and caring. Their daughter, Gudrun, came home to meet me. Once she invited me to her home in the big city, the name of which I don't recall. Gudrun was ten years older than I, single, and very sophisticated. I had a great time with her, but my loneliness for someone my age who spoke my language kept gnawing at my insides. One day, three young women walked past us as Tante Maria and I were walking to one of the coffee klatches. I heard their laughter, caught a few words, and realized that they were speaking Polish. Without even an "excuse me" to Tante Maria, I ran after them, yelling in Polish. They stopped and looked at me in astonishment, and then, without a pause, we were all jabbering at the same time. It was quickly established that they were Jewish concentration-camp survivors and were, to their knowledge, the only Poles in Landskrona. I was immediately asked to join them. As I translated our conversation to Tante Maria she gave me a big grin and said, "Go."

As usual, I made an immediate connection with one of the girls, who was eighteen years old. Her name was Dora Schwartz and she was from eastern Poland; one of the other two was also from that part of the country. The third girl was from Czechoslovakia, and because her language was similar to Polish we had no trouble communicating. I had just found another nuclear family. The girls lived in a room on the grounds of a hospital, where they worked in the kitchen. We became inseparable. I saw them every day after they were through with work.

One day they asked whether I was going to the synagogue for Rosh Hashanah services, a holiday that I had a memory of someplace in the deep recesses of my mind. Wanting to belong, I said, "Of course." I went home and piously informed the Larsgards that it was a Jewish holiday, and that I was supposed to fast. They respected my decision. That evening I met my friends and we went to the synagogue, where we sat upstairs in the balcony with the other women. I didn't understand a word, so I watched my friends, standing up and sitting down when they did, and pretending to read the prayer book. At last the service ended and we left. They suggested that the next morning I come to their room and once again we would all go together to the morning service. I agreed. In the morning I was very hungry, but knowing that I was supposed to fast I left home on an empty stomach. When I entered my friends' room they were eating breakfast. There was bread, sardines, cheeses, and salami, quite a feast. I was offered food. Why not? If they were eating and it was OK, why shouldn't I? So I did. About a week or so later came the question: "Do you want to come to our room and we'll go together to the service?" Without hesitation I agreed. I searched my mind, and a little spark of memory whispered to me, *Remember, this is Yom Kippur.* I ate a big dinner, then met them and went to services; likewise, the next morning I ate a hearty breakfast before meeting the girls. Later in the day I found out that they had not eaten because this was indeed the day of fasting. I was learning about my religion!

A couple of months later the hospital, which had been used for sick and contagious concentration-camp survivors, closed down. My friends lost their jobs and were being transferred to different cities across Sweden. Fortunately for me, Dora went to work in a factory in Malmö, a city that was close to Landskrona, and where I managed to visit her a couple of times. She lived in a dormitory with probably a hundred or more women. We shared her bed but there was no privacy. She had many new friends. She had also met an American pilot who'd been shot down during the war and had escaped to Sweden, and was now waiting for a ship so that he could go home to the United States. He told Dora that it would be years before I could go to America. He had good reason to think so, but then he didn't know my aunt and uncle and their determination to bypass the quotas and have me with them.

Fast and furious, letters were going back and forth across the Atlantic. Unkie and Ciocia had contacted every Jewish agency, and were told that there was a long waiting list and that I had to wait my turn. They were informed that it was impossible to get me out of Europe. Ciocia then took a different approach. She decided to bypass all the Jewish resources and proceeded to write letters to Oregon's representatives and senators. She begged them for help. I am not absolutely certain, but I believe that she also wrote to President Truman.

The impossible did happen. Toward the end of September, 1945, Uncle Nels took me to a government agency in Göteborg. We spent a few days doing I didn't know what, since I couldn't understand a word and wasn't worldly enough to know a thing about passports and visas. Approximately a month later we received a large packet in the mail. It contained everything I needed for travel to America. By mid-November we were on the way to Oslo, Norway, where we spent a few days sightseeing. Uncle Nels showed me the residence palace of the King of Norway and all kinds of beautiful places. After a few days he took me to the docks, where I boarded the SS *Stavangerfjord*. Uncle Nels came aboard with me and made sure that I was comfortable in my cabin. Soon it was time for us to sail and he had to disembark. I stood on the deck crying and waving to him, until he disappeared.

Chapter Eight

OUT OF THE ASHES

1945–1946

I was on the very first ship to leave Norway for the Americas after World War II. I even made it out of Europe before Dora's American pilot. Dora had come to Landskrona for the last weekend before my trip. She told me that she planned to go to Palestine, and we swore eternal love and friendship. To my best recollection we exchanged one letter after I arrived in America. After that she never responded.

When the land was no longer in sight, I went below to my cabin. My cabin mate, whom I had already met, was unpacking her suitcase. She was much older than I — probably in her mid-forties — and spoke only Swedish. We communicated with hand gestures. She let me know that she had taken the lower bunk, and I nodded my head in agreement. That was the first and last contact between us. The space was too small for both of us to be there at the same time. It might have been four feet by six, or maybe even smaller.

At the end of the narrow hall was a communal bathroom with showers and toilets. We were traveling steerage, at the very bottom of the ship. They referred to it as third class. Above us were the second-class and first-class levels, which I never saw, filled with Americans returning home. We were not allowed to go up there.

Soon after sailing, I learned that I was one of nearly five hundred teenagers traveling third-class to the Americas. All of us were war orphans and concentration-camp survivors, and we never mixed with the other third-class passengers. The one exception to the rule was a few Norwegian boys about eighteen to twenty years old, who were very interested in some of the survivor girls. As usual I made a connection, this time with two sisters who were going to live with an aunt and uncle in Costa Rica. Following my now well-established pattern of making quick friendships, we became a threesome. They were much more mature than I and had a wonderful time flirting with the Norwegian boys. I don't know how it happened, but one of the boys liked me. I had a boyfriend!

Many firsts occurred on that ship. I had my first menstrual period, with no idea how to take care of myself. I had my first boyfriend — Alf Hansen — and the two of us trothed eternal love. It was my first ocean voyage, and also it was the first time since 1941 that I had seen such a variety of wonderful food. The food in Sweden had been adequate, but they had food rationing, which had meant that I ate fish at least twice a day. Aboard the ship we had a smorgasbord buffet laden with a plethora of wondrous dishes, including my favorite, deviled eggs!

Halfway through our voyage, we found ourselves in the midst of a raging Atlantic storm. Everyone else became seasick, but my friends and I were fine. For about three days there were only fifteen or twenty of us in the dining room. As the boat rolled from side to side, our plates slid from one end of the table to the other. The Norwegian boys convinced my friends and me that the best way not to get seasick was to go to the bar to drink alcoholic beverages and smoke cigarettes; there was no age limit on either drinking or smoking. Trying hard to appear worldly and sophisticated, I agreed, but in fact that was the closest I came to being seasick and nauseous.

At last, after about ten days of seeing nothing but the ocean, someone yelled from the deck: "I see something in the distance! I think it's New York!" Drenched by the downpour of rain, with the howling wind whipping through our clothing, most of the five hundred of us stood on the deck holding onto the railings and each other, and peering out at the horizon. I could barely breathe as slowly, slowly, the ship moved ahead. Through the dense fog of the night I saw buildings, and a lighted Statue of Liberty welcoming us to the land of the free.

Freedom! What a feeling! What an incredible sight! I stood there with tears pouring down my cheeks, tasting their salt mixed with the brine of the ocean. As though we were all one, a thunderous ovation escaped from all of our lips: "America! America!!!"

We had to wait until the next morning to disembark. I tearfully said goodbye to my boyfriend, Alf, and to my two girlfriends, who were going to Costa Rica and were not allowed to leave the ship. Even though I was very excited, it was extremely difficult to part from my new friends. To the best of my knowledge I was the only one of the five hundred teenage survivors to get off the ship in the United States. Once again I felt a tremendous sense of loss and loneliness, as I stepped into a room and went through a line of officials who inspected all my documents.

A man handed me an envelope that was addressed to me. He said, "Welcome to America," and pointed me toward the gangplank. Along the way I stopped to read the contents of my envelope. Handwritten by Unkie was a message: "We couldn't come aboard the ship — they wouldn't let us — but we will be waiting for you at the bottom of the gangplank. We can hardly wait to see you. Love, Uncle Moniek and Ciocia Hanita."

I took off at a trot, until I saw them standing there waiting for me. The reality of the situation penetrated through my emotional haze. This was my new life! At last I was safe. I was loved and wanted. I was home. It was over. I fell into their loving outstretched arms.

After a million and one kisses we were inside a taxicab, with me surrounded by Unkie on one side and Ciocia on the other. We held hands all the way to our hotel. I was overwhelmed by the outpouring of their love. Every so often, Unkie would let go of my hand and stroke my cheek, all the time murmuring endearments in Polish. "*Moja lalka*" and "*Kizuhna*" were his favorite expressions, "My dolly" and "Kitten." Squeezed between the two of them, I couldn't see much out of the taxi windows, but I still managed to get the flavor of New York, hearing the cacophony of automobile horns and feeling my body sliding from one side to the other as our taxi driver brazenly wove in and out of traffic.

Welcome to New York! I behaved as if I had been there before. Nothing surprised me; Unkie pointed out the revolving doors and was taken aback when I told him that they were common in Sweden. I was not, however, prepared for an American hotel. In Sweden and Norway, Uncle Nels and I had stayed in small, shabby rooms; in one hotel we had had to walk up four stories to our room, while another had a two-person elevator that squeaked its way up and down at a snail's pace.

Our taxi stopped, and a man dressed in a fancy uniform stepped forward and opened the cab door for us. We had arrived at the Taft Hotel, and now I could not help revealing my amazement: the lobby was spacious and beautifully appointed with crystal chandeliers and opulent furnishings, all surrounded by an open mezzanine.

In the room I unpacked my meager possessions, and then Ciocia took me down to the soda fountain inside the hotel. I had no idea what to order. My English was less than minimal, even though in Sweden I had read several books in English in an effort to learn the language. Ciocia ordered a cherry soda for me. It was the most delicious thing I have ever had in my whole life!

After that I was told that a family was coming to the hotel to talk with me. On the mezzanine, we met a man, his wife, and their teenage daughter. The wife was the sister of Aunt Nadzia; she and Nadzia were my mother's cousins. She bombarded me with one question after another, which Unkie translated from English to Polish, reversing the process to translate my Polish into English for them. I had no answers. Her sister, Nadzia, had lived with her husband in Aleksandrow; their son, Adaś, had been my cousin and playmate. Aunt Nadzia, a dentist, had been very worldly. In 1939 she had visited her sister in New York, but had returned home despite the looming war in Europe. Apparently she could have stayed in the United States, but she had refused to abandon her husband and son in Poland. They were very integrated into Polish society, and she was convinced that everything that was happening to Jews would not affect her and her family. So they remained in their home country.

Aunt Nadzia's sister could neither understand nor accept the fact that there was no way for me to have knowledge of what happened to any of our extended family. Looking bewildered, she kept saying, "But your mother was so very close to Nadzia." At that early date, so soon after the war, very few Americans really understood what had transpired in Europe. Eventually our visitors left.

Although I didn't have any information about what had happened to the various members of our extended family, I tried to talk to Unkie about the fates of our immediate family. I wanted him to know what I had been through, as well as what had happened to all of them — where and when they had died, the approximate dates of their murders. I had barely started to speak, when he said, "Don't talk about it! It is all behind you. You are here with us; you are safe. Don't talk about it!" And so, feeling lucky that I was wanted, loved, and accepted by him, I stopped trying to talk about the past.

We stayed in New York for about a week. We shopped for proper American clothes for me. They took me to shows and restaurants. Every time I said anything about my experiences, I was silenced by: "Don't talk about it!" Uncle Moniek did not want to hear anything about what had happened to my mother and father and grandparents — to his sister and brother-in-law, his parents.

I felt safe and loved, and really fell in love with my Ciocia, who truly became my second mother. After a very busy and adventuresome time in New York we boarded the *City of Roses* for the cross-country trip to Portland. The train ride took a few days, and we arrived in Portland at the break of dawn. Standing on the platform to greet us was a couple with two little girls. It was Ciocia's brother, Adolf Asher, and his wife and two daughters, Joan, age eight, and Evelyn, age five. They were introduced to me as Uncle Adolf, Aunt Dorothy, and my cousins. As if by magic, I had a whole new family. Evelyn and I had an instant love affair. We left the train depot and the whole family, all seven of us, went to celebrate my arrival at a breakfast in the restaurant of the Portland Hotel. Evie sat next to me. We held hands and I had to cut her French toast. That breakfast was the beginning of my new life.

I couldn't talk about the war that was my past. I had sworn to live and to be happy if I survived. The only way I knew to defeat Hitler — and to avenge the murder of my parents and grandparents and all of my cousins, aunts, and uncles — was to live a happy and fulfilling life. I had to live my life for all of them. From that point on I decided to put the past behind me.

I worked very hard to become a typical American teenager. My English was very poor and I had a heavy accent. Many of the kids were uncomfortable around me; no matter how hard I tried, I was different. They couldn't understand me. I ignored this problem and kept chattering away. Eventually I met a girl, Estelle Bachman, who wasn't afraid of my differences and wanted to be my friend. We became best friends.

Through Estelle and her brother, Alfie, I met many other teenagers. Estelle's mother treated me as though I was her own daughter. Slowly my body and soul were being nurtured back to good health. The summer of 1946 was a time in my life that I have never forgotten. We had parties and dances and weekly picnics at most of the city parks. My favorite was Macleay Park, with its icy streams to hold our watermelons, and its miles of pristine hiking trails.

I accomplished my goal. Suppressing my memories of the war years, whenever I spoke of my childhood I told tales of that glorious time before the war.

I was happy.

Epilogue

TALKING ABOUT IT

1970–2010

One day in 1970, I answered the phone. A man asked if I was Mrs. Greenstein, and I said that I was. He told me that he was fundraising for the American Nazi Party, and asked me for a donation. When I replied, "I am not interested in donating to your party," his voice became threatening and obscenities poured out of his mouth. He ended his tirade by calling me a filthy, rotten Jew and said, "We are going to get you and yours! We'll burn your house down! We'll get you!" Then he hung up.

I stood there speechless and terrified. He had managed to transport me back to the horrors of the concentration camps. Shaking like a leaf, I called Tole. He was with a patient and couldn't leave his office. He calmed me down and said to call the police. I followed his instructions, and spoke to the police as well as to an FBI agent. They were wonderful, and for a time provided a special patrol to watch our house.

The terror had returned, but I couldn't let my children see it. I didn't want them to inherit my fear. Tole and I informed them of the incident and told them to be observant and aware of anything different in our neighborhood. Nothing happened, and I am sure that my daughters have no memory of that event.

In 1987, swastikas and graffiti appeared on the walls of businesses in southeast Portland, in the area surrounding Cleveland High School, the school from which all four of my girls had graduated. Skinheads were becoming a common sight in that neighborhood. I was upset and quite nervous, but continued to ignore the situation until one terrible evening in 1988. On November 13th, an Ethiopian student at Portland State University was murdered by racist skinheads while walking on a street maybe a mile from where I lived. His name was Mulugeta Seraw. He was a mere twenty years old, and had come to our country in pursuit of higher education. He was not involved in gangs or any other illegal activities. His crime was the color of his skin!

I remember hearing about this horrible event on the evening news; his murder was also reported in the *Oregonian* newspaper. I was shaken and outraged by this stupid act of hatred. I recall thinking that something had to be done. *Who can do it? Where do I call?* Suddenly I realized that I was expecting someone else to take steps on my behalf. But who would express the outrage I felt? A paraphrase of a quotation popped into my head: *If not I, then who? If not now, then when?"*

Shortly thereafter I joined the speakers bureau at the newly formed Oregon Holocaust Resource Center. Unkie and Ciocia were dead. Tole had died in 1985. All four of my girls were married and had children of their own. Not having Jewish-sounding last names, they were safe. At last, silence would no longer suffice. It was time for me to talk about it!

My first speaking assignment was at Cleveland High School. Of all the possibilities, who would have thought that my first time would be at the school my own children had attended! I worried and fretted about the students' sensibilities. How do I tell them about my experiences during the Holocaust? I decided to be gentle, and not too graphic in my descriptions. But when I asked the teacher for some feedback a few days later, he said that the students had thought that, compared to Anne Frank, what I had been through was not so bad. The next time I spoke I didn't try to tone things down, and told my story straight out. The fifty eighth-graders were spellbound. From then on I have always treated the students as adults.

I spoke at middle schools, high schools, universities, to high-school assemblies of as many as seven hundred students. I spoke at juvenile correctional institutions, state prisons, federal prisons. In 1992 we brought an exhibition about the life of Anne Frank to Portland, which was so popular that a smaller version of it was created to travel around Oregon over the following year. Every local Holocaust survivor who was willing to speak about his or her experiences was invited to join the speakers group; during that year I must have spoken two or three times a week, sometimes traveling two hundred miles a day. I even journeyed to Alaska to speak at youth groups and prisons in Anchorage and at schools and other venues in Juneau.

By 1994, all that talking brought on frequent nightmares, in bright Technicolor. In the middle of one night I got out of bed and found an empty canvas and my painting supplies. I set a small easel on the counter of my kitchen island, and furiously proceeded to slash paint all over the canvas. My memories of the Holocaust were pouring forth. I painted nonstop for months, never knowing what might come out of me. My paintings were a work of my subconscious, emotions and memories buried deep under the veneer of culture and sophistication.

Now, as I write this, I am rapidly approaching old age. So far, I am still continuing to speak at schools and various other venues, and I serve as a docent for the Oregon Holocaust Memorial. Thousands of people visit our Memorial every year, including organized tours for students. For the past twenty-two years my mission has been to educate people, primarily young people, about intolerance and its consequences. I talk about the awful things that occurred, but I also tell them about the acts of kindness.

I throw a little pebble into a still pool of water, in the hope that the ripples it creates reach the shores of acceptance and respect.

Afterword

Marshall M. Lee

Ten-year-old Miriam Kominkowska had no way of knowing how precarious was the state of her world, indeed the future of her very life. As a Polish Jew in 1939 she was about to become one of the most endangered people on earth. Her world had already begun to turn upside down. Yet, of politics and war what does any ten-year-old know?

Flat and essentially featureless, Poland is a handful of grain lying between two great millstones: Germany to the west and Russia to the east. And, as the grain, from 1939 until 1990 Poland would be ground to powder between these two great forces. By far the more enduring of the forces was the Soviet Union, whose suzerainty Poland endured from 1945 until 1990. By far the more violent, barbaric, and lethal, however, was the German occupation under which Poland suffered for the six years from 1939 to 1945.

In 1939 Poland had a population of thirty-five million, of whom the overwhelming majority were Catholic. Among the thirty-five million were three million Polish Jews who had been a part of Polish life and culture for centuries. Anti-Semitism was common throughout Poland, for the most part casual rather than overt, for the most part tolerated by the Catholic Church and certainly reinforced by the Church's prayerful plea every Sunday to save the souls of the Jews, in the Church's view the betrayers of Christ. Far from having the assimilated status of Jews in Germany and Western Europe, Polish Jews were nevertheless economically, if not socially, integrated into Polish life. And in the smaller towns and villages of Poland, Jews such as the Kominkowskis enjoyed cordial relations with the majority of their neighbors and professional associates. Intermarriage remained rare, but particularly in the Jewish upper and middle classes, social intercourse with their gentile Polish countrymen had improved markedly over the past decades.

All this came to an abrupt end with the German invasion of Poland on September 1, 1939. Old suspicions returned, festering resentments erupted, and the German occupiers not only played on these, they immediately adopted a policy of promoting, indeed deepening, Poland's historic anti-Semitism. During the ensuing six years of ruthless occupation the Germans directly killed or indirectly promoted the death of 31.4 percent of Poland's pre-war population, the single greatest percentage loss of population of any nation during World War II. And among the eleven million Polish deaths, 2,955,000 were Jews, a staggering 98.5 percent of Poland's prewar Jewish population of three million. It was in Poland that the Germans came the closest to realizing Hitler's dream of the complete elimination of all Jews under his dominion.

It is in this forsaken landscape that the innocent Miriam Kominkowska found herself. At the end of the war she was among the 1.5 percent of Poland's Jews to have survived. By some combination of luck, inner strength, and daring Miriam made it out alive. What had she been up against? How long were the odds? From the distance of six and a half decades it is impossible to imagine. In a certain sense, it is hard to see how forty-five thousand Jews survived.

In late August 1939, as he prepared to pounce on a hapless Poland, Hitler secretly agreed to divide his catch with the Soviet Union. Within the context of a Russo-German non-aggression pact, Hitler obtained Stalin's agreement to stand aside while Germany invaded Poland, in exchange for granting Stalin the eastern half of the country. For his part, Stalin was delighted to put as much additional territory between Germany and the

Soviet Union as he could. By the end of September 1939, Germany had conquered and occupied the western half of Poland, and Soviet troops had occupied the eastern Polish territories. And so it would remain until June 1941.

Germany immediately annexed the northern and westernmost Polish territories into Germany proper. Interestingly, until she and her mother were transported to Auschwitz, young Miriam Kominkowska and her family resided within the confines of the newly enlarged East Prussia, and then during the Łodz ghetto period in the Warthegau, both new parts of Germany proper. The central and southern Polish territories became what was known as the General Government, whose overseer was one of the Nazi Party's highest-ranking officials, Hans Frank. As events would unfold, this area, where four of the six killing centers of the Holocaust were located, was in the part of Poland controlled by the Nazi Party itself.

Almost immediately following the end of the Polish campaign, German authorities dispatched special teams whose mission was to round up and to liquidate the political, intellectual, and cultural leaders of Poland. In every city and town, every village and hamlet, these teams, which became the nucleus of the *Einsatzgruppen* of 1941, hunted down teachers and priests, labor leaders and politicians, business leaders and intellectuals, mayors and librarians, professors and retired military officers. It made no difference whether these victims were Catholics or Jews; Germany's aim was, in effect, to liquidate Poland's central nervous system, leaving only its skeleton and muscles for agricultural and industrial labor. The party opportunists and profiteers arrived to manage matters in Poland, and behind them came German peasant settlers to displace the native rural population.

At the same time that Germany set out to colonize Poland, German authorities began to round up Germany's Jews and dispatch them east to restricted zones in Poland. The ghettoization of German and

Polish Jews had begun. With several exceptions, Łodz being the most significant, virtually all of these ghettoes could be found in the General Government area of Poland. In the spring of 1940 German forces overran Denmark, Norway, Holland, Luxembourg, Belgium, and France. By year's end Jews from Germany's newly conquered territories began to arrive in the already choked and disease-ridden ghettoes of the Warthegau and General Government Poland.

At first, officials in Berlin glibly anticipated that overcrowding in the ghettoes, combined with starvation-level food allowances and virtually no medical arrangements, would lead to a "natural winnowing" of the weakest elements of the captive population. This sanguinary Darwinism fueled the confident predictions among SS and party leaders that the Jews would rapidly die off from such neglect. When they did not perish quickly enough, nerves in both the Warthegau and Berlin began to fray.

By mid-1941, with ghettoes bursting at the seams, disease rampant in and around the ghettoes, and more Jews arriving every day, local Nazi officials, in conjunction with local SS administrators in cities and districts in the Warthegau and General Government Poland, began to take matters into their own hands. And now, as Germany invaded Russia in late June 1941, traversing the eastern half of the former Poland, the prospect of more than a million additional Jews in the General Government alone overwhelmed not only the thinking but the imagination of occupation authorities in Poland.

And so it was that in the fall of 1941, flushed with their astonishing initial military successes in the East, German officials in the field began to improvise a solution for their local problems of overcrowding and disease. Yet, even as the local and regional SS and police officials experimented with killing Jews using technology borrowed from Germany's euthanasia program of the late Thirties — gas vans at Chelmno, not far from Łodz, and stationary carbon monoxide installations at several locations along the Bug River east of Warsaw — initiatives were under way in Berlin that would lead to the industrial murder of the Jews. Already in July, Hermann Göring, in his capacity as titular head of the national police administration, had issued orders to SS Chief Heinrich Himmler for the "Final Solution of the Jewish Question." Without hesitation Himmler followed up Göring's orders with orders of his own to his second in command, Reinhard Heydrich. Heydrich, in turn, dispatched his trusted lieutenant Adolf Eichmann to Poland early that fall to report on conditions in the field.

What Eichmann found was a welter of overlapping jurisdictions and authorities, ad hoc experiments bred of desperation and a lack of clear leadership from the center in Berlin. Not only did these experiments entail various methods from the euthanasia program, but at the Auschwitz labor camp in Upper Silesia, about an hour's drive from Krakow, the camp commandant had begun to experiment with the use of a powerful commercial cyanide-based fumigant, Zyklon-B, having sealed up an outbuilding at the camp and murdered almost a thousand Russian POWs. But Eichmann learned something else while in the East, something that had already begun to trouble authorities far from the front at their desks in Berlin.

As German troops advanced into Russia in three great army groups they were followed closely by four highly mobile "special action teams," or *Einsatzgruppen*. Comprising SS and police troops, motorized and equipped with the most advanced communications equipment, the four *Einsatzgruppen* had as their assignment to round up and shoot all the Jews they could find behind the advancing German forces. And they were spectacularly successful. Between the late summer of 1941, and early 1943 when the *Einsatzgruppen* were disbanded, the several thousand *Einsatzgruppen* members managed to kill well in excess of a million Jews and tens of thousands of Soviet political "enemies." Such success, however, was impossible without the direct assistance of regular army units and the cooperation of local residents. In other words, the grisly work of the *Einsatzgruppen* was hardly a secret. Indeed, as early as the late fall of 1941 regular army troops began to write home about what they had witnessed, and by early 1942 troops on leave brought photographs home documenting events "in the East."

To officials in Berlin the roadside shootings of Jews in the Baltic States and the Ukraine posed a number of problems: not only did news get out of these atrocities and the increasing role of alcohol among troops assigned to do the shooting, but the enthusiasm of local populations proved unnerving. Often word spread of an "action" and entire families would turn out, picnic in hand, to watch the murderous work of the Jews' executioners. So, under the guise of contending with the stress suffered by the executioners themselves, Himmler and his lieutenants determined in the late fall of 1941 to regularize the ad hoc local initiatives in the Warthegau and General Government Poland.

Still, despite these efforts at the center, no one system prevailed. The overriding concern seems to have been ease of transport, so killing centers flourished near the most populous ghettoes. Chelmno near Łodz, as well as the camps in the Bug River system — Treblinka, Sobibor, and Belzec — all employed various carbon monoxide systems first used in the euthanasia program. At the same time, at Majdanek, a mile from Lublin, and at Auschwitz and Auschwitz Birkenau, the Zyklon-B method prevailed. All these camps grew and reached full capacity in 1942. That year also marked a complete year of murder by the *Einsatzgruppen* in the Soviet Union. In 1943 the *Einsatzgruppen* were phased out, and in November, as the year came to a close, the last large-scale shooting operation, *Erntefest*, or Spring Harvest, took place as German police troops tried to eliminate all remaining Jews in the General Government's jurisdiction. Since Miriam Kominkowska remained in the Łodz ghetto in the Warthegau, she fell outside the scope of *Erntefest*.

Although Miriam escaped the *Erntefest* by virtue of being interred in the Łodz ghetto, her circumstances soon worsened with her transport to Auschwitz Birkenau. By 1944 the Auschwitz complex was the largest cluster of camps within the German concentration-camp system. It was a multi-purpose camp, as was Majdanek. And while more people, just over one million, were murdered at Auschwitz than at any other single camp, it was by no means the deadliest camp, a distinction that falls to Chelmno, from which only two people are known to have survived. If Chelmno was tiny and exceptionally deadly, in comparison Auschwitz was a gigantic planet of death.

The Auschwitz Main Camp — Auschwitz I — was a tightly confined several acres of multi-storied red-brick buildings, which had formerly housed an Austrian army artillery base. Chosen by Himmler in 1940 to become the center of a vast agricultural resettlement area in Upper Silesia, Auschwitz was initially to provide the slave labor for a host of projects in the region. It rapidly expanded as political prisoners filled the Main Camp site.

By 1941 initial construction began for a second camp, several kilometers to the west: Auschwitz II, better known as Birkenau. Eventually Birkenau would grow to include four gas-chamber / crematorium buildings and more than 220 barracks buildings. As late as the winter of 1944, even as Soviet forces approached, the Germans were adding new barracks at Birkenau, following plans that projected a prisoner population in excess of half a million.

From the earliest days, Himmler intended Auschwitz to be the center of a cluster of sub-camps that would provide slave labor to industry. By 1942 that was becoming a reality as numerous German companies built factories and plants nearby, necessitating the establishment of Auschwitz III at Monowitz, several kilometers east of the Auschwitz Main Camp. Thus, from the time Jews began to arrive at Auschwitz, those capable of a few months' labor might be selected to live. And it was this selection process that Miriam and her mother endured upon their arrival in 1944.

What neither had reason to know was that 1944 was the most frenzied year in the camp's short history. For it was in 1944 that Germany forced Hungary to offer up its Jewish population — the largest intact population of Jews remaining in Europe — to the German authorities. To accommodate the crush of Hungarian transports that spring and summer, rail lines had been extended into Birkenau almost to the doors of Crematoria II and III. Arriving trains would now disgorge their tortured contents onto sidings inside the camp and just a short walk from the gas chambers. Such an increase in traffic in Birkenau inevitably caused great confusion. Often prisoners selected to live were processed on arrival but not immediately assigned to a labor battalion. We get a clear glimpse of this confusion in the days after Miriam's arrival.

First assigned to a barracks in the women's camp and then eventually transferred to another in the Hungarian camp, Miriam made a journey through Birkenau that was punctuated by luck and the kindness and strength of a handful of remarkable fellow prisoners. It was fall, and operations at the camp began to wind down as the Soviet army drew closer. The Germans started to evacuate those prisoners whom they could still work to death, and by chance Miriam was among those dispatched west. These evacuations brought what for tens of thousands of prisoners was their final torture: the death marches of the winter of 1944–45. Some sixty thousand prisoners from Auschwitz were forced to march west through the snow and ice of winter to camps in Germany. Of these, fifteen thousand died in their tracks. In Miriam's case, she was spared the harrowing experience of the death marches when she and her fellow prisoners were sent by train to the concentration camp at Bergen-Belsen.

Ultimately it was in Bergen-Belsen — after first being transferred to a labor camp in Magdeburg, Germany, and then returned — that Miriam lived out her final fever-wracked days of captivity. It was here that, following liberation, she and a tiny cluster of fellow Poles supported each other and fed off one another's will to live.

The winds of peace carried this little band of survivors to Sweden, and, eventually, delivered Miriam into the waiting arms of her aunt and uncle as she arrived in New York. Yet, even as the teenage survivor embarked on a new journey — a journey to Oregon, American citizenship, and the start of a new life — the heart of a Pole remained.

Marshall M. Lee
Professor of History, Emeritus
Pacific University

Winter 2010